The Responsive Universe

The Responsive Universe
Illumination of the Nine Mandalas

John C. Bader

Wisdom Moon Publishing
2014

THE RESPONSIVE UNIVERSE
ILLUMINATION OF THE NINE MANDALAS

Copyright © 2014 Wisdom Moon Publishing, LLC

All rights reserved. Tous droits réservés.

No part of this work may be copied, reproduced, recorded, stored, or translated, in any form, or transmitted by any means electronic, mechanical, or other, whether by photocopy, fax, email, internet group postings, or otherwise, without written permission from the copyright holder, *except for brief quotations* in reviews for a magazine, journal, newspaper, broadcast, podcast, etc., or in scholarly or academic papers, *when quoted with a full citation to this work*.

Published by Wisdom Moon Publishing LLC
San Diego, CA, USA

Wisdom Moon™, the Wisdom Moon logo™, Wisdom Moon Publishing™, and WMP™ are trademarks of Wisdom Moon Publishing LLC.

www.WisdomMoonPublishing.com

ISBN 978-1-938459-28-3 (softcover, alk. paper)
ISBN 978-1-938459-35-1 (eBook)
LCCN 2014953610

Special thanks to
Kim Dzwonkowski
who helped edit my first manuscript
and continues to add eloquence to my thoughts

Table of Contents

Foreword
i

Prologue
iii

The First Mandala
Living with an Open Mind
1

The Second Mandala
The Art of Meditation
22

The Third Mandala
Religion, God, Creation and the Universe
39

The Fourth Mandala
The De-Construction of Organized Religion
57

The Fifth Mandala
Understanding the Past
82

The Sixth Mandala
Understanding Loss
95

The Seventh Mandala
Living Healthy through Mind and Body
110

The Eighth Mandala
Karma and Positive Energy
137

The Ninth Mandala
Confronting Reality Leads to Self-Actualization
162

About the Author
186

Notes
188

Foreword

We live on a unique planet of modest size, orbiting an average star in a galaxy that contains several billion other stars. Further, scattered across the vast Cosmos are billions of other galaxies home to billions more stars.

Everything tangible and intangible in the Cosmos is made of energy. Everything seen and unseen within this grand Universe is comprised of particles and waves of light and energy that are interconnected.

Instinctual consciousness is intrinsic to the Universe

This Universe is boundless in periphery; its energy and form are immeasurable; everything linked at the sub-atomic level weaves this complex tapestry that is everything.

Despite the immensity of the Cosmos, despite the far-reaching realm of space and time, there is a connective quality to all that exists. Everything is linked to this responsive field of instinctual energy. It is here in the quantum Universe that actions create reactions and energy can't be destroyed, it simply changes form.

In an interstellar dominion of noble gases, dark matter and pinpoint light, there is a responsive element that unites humans with an omnipresent link to love, wisdom, and energy. Such visions of grandeur can be overwhelming and many times unimaginable; yet, deep down there is this sublime familiarity and relationship; thoughts and experiences in life remind us that we are part of this grand concept.

From imperfection is born beauty, energy, and human perception; this is what defines the Responsive Universe and is the source of our conscious and instinctual existence.

Prologue

A common thread in this book is our need and ability to question authority and to confirm that what we learn, from societal, political, and spiritual points of view, is valid information. Just think of how science and philosophy continually evolve. At times, changes in theory are so drastic; they rewrite encyclopedias and scientific journals. The 1500s, for example, brought an amazing revolution of thinking. During the life of Polish astronomer Nicolaus Copernicus, the Church, governments, and the vast majority of people of Europe held the belief that the Earth was the center of the Universe, around which the Sun and all stars revolved. This theory was so adamantly believed that authorities punished anyone who contested it. One man, however, set the world on its heels—Italian astronomer Galileo Galilei—by proving through painstaking observation and various scientific methods that the Earth was not the center of the Universe. The Catholic Church was quick to label the theories of Galileo, Copernicus, and the like ridiculous and even blasphemous. It wasn't until March of 1984 that Pope John Paul II finally conceded and corrected a 350-year wrong.

I cite this reference to laud free minds like Galileo and Copernicus, whose challenges to their world's belief system threatened their lives. These scientists died long before we caught up and celebrated their theories as the monumental scientific discoveries they were. I can only imagine their frustration—forever fighting the ignorance and fear that ran unchallenged in the highest echelons of power. Many free thinkers still face punishment and ostracism for their beliefs today. I find comfort in imagining that Galileo and Copernicus did not waver from their theories. As long as you have faith in your beliefs, you will instill that faith into an entire system of thought that defines you as an individual. If this system of thought is authentic and aligns to your True Nature, you will evolve into something amazing and sublime.

My thoughts and the words that I write are in the spirit of free minds like Galileo and Copernicus: They constantly evolve and adapt over the course of my life as I take in more information and learn. Living is an evolutionary process of maturity and wisdom. We have to remain receptive to new information and be able to adapt and change on a daily basis. The theory that rankled the Church during Galileo's time was the idea that we were not the center of the Universe. I think that no matter what we have proven scientifically over the centuries, we still have problems accepting that the world does not, in fact, revolve around us.

After my awakening several years ago, I saw a fleeting vision of a "True Reality" where an energy force connected every atom in the Universe. In my mind's eye, I saw that God or creation is so vast and magnificent, that it is almost incomprehensible. That vastness gets distilled and made comprehensible by two-thousand-year-old parables whose interpretations by the Church rarely adapt and evolve with changing times. We are not the center of the Universe; we are merely part of something so immense it boggles the imagination.

What we should take from the likes of Copernicus and Galileo is that questioning authority and adapting thought is one of the most extraordinary gifts we have as humans. Both scientists were free thinkers in a close-minded world, but they held onto their faiths and truths, and eventually, the rest of the world caught up to them. Scientifically speaking, Earth is not the center of the Universe. Metaphorically speaking, our egos are not the center of everything either. We are all part of something far bigger than ourselves; something we can't yet explain but have tried over the centuries to describe in scriptures whose interpretations do not hold up in changing times. What we do know is that accepting the Universe's vastness and awakening to our part in its function and beauty leads us to a feeling of happiness where we feel a part of something connected and inspiring. This road to enlightenment and personal fulfillment is a long but rewarding path. It doesn't matter if you or I look back on these words with a different pair of eyes years down the road. This is where we are now on our journey in life. Each day writes new chapters, and an important part of our journey begins right now.

The Responsive Universe is a literary guide to self-discovery. The combination of learning tools, meditations, and daily life practices in this book will start you on a journey of new-found clarity and mindfulness. I openly suggest that you start a journal in conjunction with reading this book. Journaling is a great outlet and tool for expanding perspectives and keeping track of progress. *The Responsive Universe*, in fact, began as a journal. It doesn't have to be anything fancy—just have something, a notebook or a computer, so you can flesh out new perspectives when inspiration strikes.

The Responsive Universe is based on Nine Mandalas, or tiers to self-discovery. In its simplest form, mandala means "circle." It is an ancient Buddhist symbol of inner space where everything is linked as one and from which the Cosmos and all its energy arise. The mandala includes the journey of birth, life, and death. By recognizing the Nine Mandalas, I see life as an adventure in learning. The Mandalas have diminished my fears and uncertainties; with less room for fear, my life has more space for happiness and growth.

The First Mandala is about living with an open mind—questioning our schooling and challenging our current way of thinking. Are our belief systems and actions based in a true reality or are they muddled with ego, low self-esteem, and misinterpreted information? The Second Mandala teaches meditation and daily life practice. The Third and Fourth challenge organized religion and delve into spiritual matters like creation and the afterlife. The Fifth and Sixth Mandalas discuss our childhoods and pasts in an effort to understand loss and control patterns, essential to freeing ourselves from suffering. The Seventh Mandala discusses living in a healthier world, both mentally and physically. The Eighth Mandala touches on karma and positive energy, both which create and enhance our growth and happiness. And finally, the Ninth Mandala is about unity and connection, and brings our journey around full circle.

In the Second Mandala, I will introduce you to meditation. In each chapter, I will include guided meditations as well as meditation-exit exercises I call a "daily life practice." Take your time with the meditations and practices. Everyone's life has its own pace, especially with work schedules and families. Though short in page length, this book is dense with topic and will definitely be more potent to the patient reader. This book isn't meant to be a quick read; it's meant to be an inspiring and educational voyage. So take your time. And don't forget your journal.

John C. Bader

For more information, please visit **responsiveuniverse.com**

The First Mandala

Living with an Open Mind

The Aperture of an Open Mind

As complex as the human brain is, it can work in very simple ways. A colorful working analogy is the hallway closet or basement you have in your home that is filled with tattered old photographs, unique mementos, and gifts of yesteryear. You get the idea. This closet contains a collection of items from years past that you rarely use, yet somehow it all survives the annual garage sale and even that monumental move when you vowed to throw it all away. You continue to hold on to old VHS tapes in spite of the brand new Blue Ray DVD player proudly displayed in your living room. You have clothing so vintage your children ask to haul it out for Halloween. You keep family heirlooms and souvenirs because they are visual records of your past. They are tangible evidence of who you are, where you came from, and where you've been. You may sometimes even rummage through the items and take a trip down memory lane.

The mind works much like this hallway closet or basement. Our brains have billions of neurons as storage facilities for everything that has transpired in our lives—grade-school memories, parents, old girlfriends or boyfriends. Everything our minds process since birth directly relates to who we are today. It's strange that old memories will fade in the back of our minds to the point where we don't even recall bits and pieces of our pasts, yet they continue to influence our subconscious with our hard-wired behaviors. Our past dictates our present actions and also our future wellness.

While eventually it's easy to bag up and dispose or donate old items from the closet when ambition strikes, old memories are far more permanent. This analogy reminds me of pathological collectors, or "hoarders." Some people have the ability to throw away things that are no longer needed, while others, like hoarders, keep everything, letting things pile up until their homes are unlivable. Here, the mind is much like a home—people who hold onto anger, jealousy, or who cling to their ego will have a cluttered mind. Old memories of moments that altered our self-perception and continue to regulate our self-esteem create control patterns, or hard-wired behaviors we adopt unconsciously through the actions and reactions of those around us. Social immersion can also clutter the mind with memories, perceptions, and beliefs so vast and contradictory that it blurs the boundary between that is real and what isn't. Most of us believe we have a firm grasp on what is real and true, but the majority of what we learned at a young age was taught to us by others. How can we be confident that the knowledge we have is untainted by cluttered perspectives and dogma?

The popular Nature vs. Nurture argument explains that we are a product of both our genetic traits and the environment in which we were raised. The biggest difference between these two factors is that we can change our *nurturing* while our *nature* remains the same. Despite the influx of information stored in our brains over time, we have the ability to question authorities in our lives, especially as adults. We can reflect on how opinions other than our own have shaped us over time. We can listen to others, but ultimately we have the power to think and decide things for ourselves. Too often we become comfortable with habitual ways of reacting to people and experiences. Our attitudes and feelings become so fixed and automatic, they are almost impossible to break and to escape from. This is precisely why we must learn to make effective, lasting changes in our lives. To do this, we must open our minds and seek the truths in lessons and opinions presented to us, truths unclouded by perspectives other than our own.

When a theory or idea makes sense and seems perfectly rational, it is easy to adopt and incorporate it into our own personal belief systems without doing our own theoretical reasoning. To have an open mind, you have to rifle through all the ideas and memories you're hoarding and toss away the clutter that makes your life unlivable. You must identify the source of teachings that shaped you, whether that source is the media, politics, religion, school, family, or even close friends, and realize that these multiple perspectives have colored your own. This can include memories of abuse, loss, or any other suffering you have experienced and lived through. In order to determine the truths in those thoughts, theories, and ideals that act as outside influences to us, we must find the root of each idea's creation. We must peel away layers of differing perspectives to reveal the pure, unadulterated concept that breeds fresh wisdom and enlightenment. Just as time and technology have changed the geography of the earth, theories and beliefs birthed centuries ago have changed and evolved to fit society's changing needs. The parables in the New Testament, for example, are lessons in living life wisely. These parables, however, dealt with wisdom as it related to a specific culture at a specific time. As cultures change, the parables are often interpreted differently, whether in good ways or bad, to fit their present context better. The United States Constitution is another example—the founding fathers drafted the document to provide the framework for freedom and choice in the late 1700s. To date, we have amended and redefined the Constitution many times as our reality and needs change.

Just like biblical parables and old legal creeds, the belief systems that we form when we are younger may not take us smoothly into adulthood. We always hope that changes made in society and law are for the betterment of humankind, but changes made in the interest of money and power can often be negative. In much the same way, we must always be wary of how outside influences affect the growth and development of our belief systems over time. It is wise to step back and reevaluate these influences, to revisit that closet containing the relics of the past. If we do not discard the things that have discolored and decayed beyond recognition, we will be weighed down by the unnecessary. We will be anchored in place by old memories, ideas, and by opinions we don't value now, even though we subconsciously adopted them as our own long ago.

To have an open mind requires us to be comfortable with the changing landscape and contours of modern-day life. Almost everything tangible in life has an undependable quality associated with it. The phrase "undependable quality" can have an unsettling implication attached to it. But in reality change is inherent to our existence and should not have a negative connotation associated with it. For example, each day is typically different than the preceding one—there can be changes in temperature and humidity, sunny skies verses cloudy or rainy skies, or, on an even more obvious level, night versus day. Unforeseen challenges and changes always seem to greet us as we trudge through daily life. From a flat tire on the way to work to an argument with your significant other. Positive changes also greet us, like graduating college, salary increases, and unadulterated love. We as humans are constantly changing as well: We change as we age and our moods can change day to day, even hour to hour. The point is that we need to be open to change on a constant basis. People that are not comfortable or adaptable to change tend to suffer more. For some people, change can bring forth anxiety, lack of space and even fear for the unknown.

There are several key elements to living with an open mind:

- We need to be mindful of our surroundings.
- We need to be mindful of our thoughts and feelings.
- We need to be open to change in daily life.
- We need to be unafraid of the unknown.
- We need to be open to new ideas.
- We need to re-evaluate our old belief systems and discard the archaic.
- We need to be open to unforeseen challenges.
- We should not persecute others for their differing beliefs.

Self-Actualization

We all surround ourselves with familiar objects, pictures, and furniture to make up our personal environments and feel at home. We feel comfortable at home, even if our bedrooms are a mess. Just as we become accustomed to the environments in which we live, we also become accustomed to people, events, problems, and even impossible situations. Struggles and challenges become so familiar that they become permanent fixtures in our lives. They become control patterns that are difficult to break. Until we understand who we are at a spiritual, emotional, and intellectual level, we will never achieve self-actualization.

Self-actualization is the need to fully develop one's potential talents and capabilities. It is the desire to know and understand. In his book, *Hierarchy of Needs*, Abraham Maslow describes an imaginary pyramid that begins with physiological needs at its base and aesthetic principles of self-directed growth at its apex. The pyramid puts our human needs in order: At the foundation are biological needs such as eating, hydration and warmth. Safety, love, and self-esteem issues follow. After filling these needs, the desire for self-actualization becomes strong as the desire to know and understand our surroundings takes precedence in order to achieve enlightened fulfillment. Though the final destination is the same, everyone achieves enlightened fulfillment via their own road. We attain answers to life's questions according to our own cultures, methods, and needs.

People have two sources of empowerment in them—the ego and our True Nature. The first source clings to safety and familiarity out of fear. This source causes regression. It causes someone to hang onto the past. This person feels a reluctance to grow or to take chances. This person often ends up destroying what he or she already has. This source, due to inertia, is easy to follow, but it most often leads to a life that is empty, full of mediocrity and unanswered questions; hence the "material world" many of us unknowingly live within.

*Self-actualization is an illumination
of energy and wisdom*

The other source of empowerment compels us to use our abilities and confidence to strive for what we believe in and what we want in our lives. This path is more difficult to follow because it requires an open and questioning mind. This path, however, can lead you to self-discovery and enlightenment—your own personal utopia. In order to walk this path, you must tear down your current foundations built from false perceptions that other people have handed you over the years. You must rebuild your belief systems using a fresh blueprint that continually evolves, constructing an open-minded future.

The Ego

Humans relate to opposites in life: man and woman, night and day, heaven and hell. What about ego and True Nature? The ego is part of our mental devices that experiences and reacts to the outside world and thus mediates between the primitive drives of our being and the demands of the social and physical environment. The ego has many shortcomings in the ways it interprets reality. The first thing to understand is that the ego is merely an attachment that feeds off of human emotions. It is easy to understand the ego as a separate entity, a false-self, yet the ego is an integral part of the social human existence. Much like a mosquito feeds off the blood of a mammal, the ego feeds off of our fears and fantasies, and regulates our self-esteem. Self-esteem is a person's overall evaluation or appraisal of his or her own worth. For better or worse, the ego thrives on ideals, beliefs, and laws that determine a perception of the world and life that is larger than the individual. It becomes the governing force from which we unknowingly base our daily actions. It drives our self-esteem from a less-than-authentic source of empowerment. Somewhere on the road of life, the ego took up a management status in our minds and now often controls facets of every step we take.

"To be yourself in a world that is constantly trying to make you something else is the greatest accomplishment."

Ralph Waldo Emerson

Born at a premature age, the ego incorporates the various ideals and beliefs that make up our surroundings as it relates to what others think and project. It is a complex array of sources that creates an ego, from the unattainable benchmark set by celebrities to the materialistic urges brought forth by our peers and the advertising we are inundated with daily. It deals with social acceptance in communal arenas and the moral and mainstream pressures of life. In the "material world," the ego unknowingly gains power from these sources and we as malleable creatures inherit control patterns that subconsciously dictate our actions and reactions in life. Control patterns are subliminal, hard-wired urges and intentions that are controlled by the ego and facilitate and reinforce the emotions of fear, anger, jealousy and low self-worth, many times unknowingly.

There is a lot of confusion surrounding the existence or concept of an ego. I have overheard many prominent spiritual and wellness advocates say that we do not need an ego—that the ego is unnecessary. Many of us are born into a world where social Darwinism defines our existence. The ego was necessary for the early evolution of humans competing and foraging to survive, and it is necessary in the early development of children today. Though its mechanisms are crude, the ego is an unavoidable social phenomenon. Now, imagine if a child lives totally alone and isolated from social interaction; he or she may not develop an ego as we know it. But that is not going to help in social human evolution. This child will remain like an animal never progressing or evolving. The ego is basically a bi-product of our social existence.

It was not until more recently—the last 3,000-5,000 years—that humans have began searching for self-actualization. This is when modern religion was born and it is when humans began to cross the threshold of a physiological-needs-based society to an aesthetic-needs-based society. Still, the ego remains rooted into our mental facilities growing and maturing as we progress into adulthood. The ego becomes this borderless entity that is so interwoven into the fabric of our minds that we do not even realize its influence.

The Great Ego Paradox

In Buddhism we are told to treat all thoughts and emotions equally. Doing so keeps the pendulum of energy and experience from swinging too far into self-gratifying bliss or the opposite, pain and suffering. In essence we are asked to find a middle ground in how we interpret our thoughts and emotions so we are balanced—only then can the indestructible quality of our existence arise from the ashes of ego and false-self.

The paradox is this: How would we know where the middle ground is without already knowing the extreme opposites of bliss and suffering. We need to have a matrix in place that takes in consideration all facets: Self-gratifying bliss as it relates to our false-self, suffering as it relates to our false-self, and this elusive middle ground called enlightenment. When we are born, society soon hands us our ego. True, the ego is not found in the womb—the ego is man-made and in order to evolve socially it is a necessary function in our lives. It is also true that most Buddhists would contend that the ego is not a part of us—it is merely a distortion. Still, even distortions are tangible evidence of who we are (at least in some limited facet). When we look in a mirror, that image may be a distortion of our true-self—a mirrored copy that is not real, but still it is rather difficult to deny that this image is not us. As stated, we need the ego to evolve so that we can first reach the necessary milestones in Maslow's hierarchy of needs: The ego and our basic instincts feed subsistence strategies, food, and warmth, for example; only then can we begin to tackle self-actualization at the apex of self-directed growth. The concept of an ego is in itself a point of reference in societal evolution. Whether we need the ego or not is really not the point—the ego exists whether we like it or not. The focus is not to say we do not need the ego but to acknowledge that it exists and then separate its faculties or functions within our mind, to make space for it so that when thoughts and emotions arise we can distinguish which ones are proactive to our evolution and development and which ones are merely there to create false-self and ultimately suffering. We cannot deny the ego but must find awareness of its power and also its weakness. In the search for enlightenment, the key is to limit its authority and influence so that true authentic empowerment can arise from within.

The False-Self

As stated, the ego is this unavoidable social phenomenon that though necessary for early primitive human development becomes this false-self that many times unknowingly governs our thoughts, actions and reactions. Earlier we discussed the analogy of looking in the mirror and seeing a distortion of our true-self. Forged emotions like fear and anger seem like they are part of us but in reality they are merely false representations of our true-self. The ego is considered a distinguishable entity but the thoughts, emotions, and actions it projects are merely an aberration of your true unadulterated self. In the effort to be more mindful of the ego, let's explore some of the ego's more common maladies and passing defilements.

Self-gratification

Self-gratification is a big factor that reinforces our ego. Self-gratification is the act of pleasing oneself or of satisfying one's desires. There is a sexual connotation to this phrase but really self-gratification can include many things that satiate us in the moment but tend to lead to suffering in the long term. Some examples would include drinking alcohol or doing drugs. Both are vices that make us feel good in the moment but there tends to be a side effect to such indulgences, including hangovers, poor decisions, and dependency. Food is a huge self-gratifying vice. Imagine how many New Year's resolutions involve diets and even exercise. Overeating and or simply eating comfort foods that are not good for our health cause a lot of suffering, mostly in the long-term. Lack of exercise complicates things further. Being overweight or out of shape can cause short-term suffering which can effect self-esteem and health. Heart disease and diabetes would be considered long-term suffering. Co-dependency is another form of self-gratification that leads to suffering: Needing the comfort, approval or attention of someone or a group of people leads to lower self-esteem, which is a debilitating form of suffering. The problem is that we become comfortable with our life styles, which are laden with such desires. With the internet and credit cards, fast food and diet pills, everything is now at our finger tips and our egos question us as to why we would suffer by not indulging in something enjoyable—after all, we deserve it, right? It is a paradox of sorts. By NOT indulging in self-gratifying things we think we love, we suffer in the now but tend not to suffer later. It is the direct opposite for someone who self-indulges as they get immediate satisfaction and it is later that a quality of suffering is realized. This tends to create a new paradox: In order not to suffer you need to suffer a little. This is why the ego has so much control, because if we are going to suffer either way, we might as well live for the moment and worry about suffering later. That is the mentality of western culture—buy it now and pay for it later. We see it with raging credit debt on a personal level and we see governments like the United States burdened with soaring deficits and dwindling cash flow. Even our role models overspend and self-indulge. It is no wonder the ego has so much control over our wellbeing and happiness.

Material Self-Esteem

Basing your happiness on things that are not guaranteed or constant, like money or possessions, can also deeply affect self-esteem and contentment. Self-esteem is complex—it grows and shrinks with the highs and lows of life and, like the ego, often forms attachments that are not productive to things like possessions and social acceptance. Even as children we already base our self-worth largely on what our peers think of us. Our self-esteem grows better or worse as adolescence layers our lives with successes, failures, goals, and fears. We take our self-esteem and all its layers with us into adulthood, where even as parents we continue to value other people's opinions of us. Our self-esteem hinges on our level of success, our receding hairlines, our weight gain since high school, and even our children's successes. We often base our self-worth on the collective benchmark set by magazines, television, and pop culture; almost always unknowingly.

High self-esteem in this type of arena, while perhaps immediately gratifying, is counterproductive. Suppose you have the trimmings of fame, all of the luxuries and possessions you think make you great, and you lose it all one day? Will you still have your affluent friends? Will you still feel fulfilled and rich without your reputation and glory? Material self-esteem and happiness based on money, status, and possessions are empty and fleeting. It is unwise to base your happiness on things outside of you, things that are not guaranteed or constant.

Control Patterns

It is amazing how our emotions and actions seem clear to us on the outside, but once we take the time to be mindful and analyze our behavior, especially in meditation, we discover a lack of clarity in our decisions. Many of our actions are interwoven into a metaphorical web of dysfunction, all of which we can trace back to control patterns that most likely started in childhood. Control patterns are unconscious behaviors that are hard-wired or mentally engrained into your mind. We often unknowingly react or exhibit a specific emotion or fear based on experiences we had earlier in life. Where does anger arise from? Where do anxiety and inhibition arise from? All of our control patterns that we many times unknowingly possess are born from an earlier time in life. Here is a basic example: We have all seen this at the grocery store: A mother and child in line ahead of you, the child begging for a bag of candy. At first the mother says no and stands firm. The child cries harder and starts a tantrum. Overwhelmed and embarrassed, the mother capitulates, handing over the candy, just to make the tantrum stop. Repetition of this and similar patterns will eventually condition the child to think that in order to get something he or she wants; all that is needed is a well-timed tantrum.

Each action and experience over time creates an unconscious memory bank of mind patterns that resurface later as control patterns. Transactional Analysis is one of the most accessible theories that sheds light on control patterns. Founded by Eric Berne, the theory suggests that the human brain acts like a tape recorder. Over time, we may forget experiences, but our brain has them recorded. Along with event details, our brain also records the feelings associated with each experience. Both the feelings and events stay locked together and create control patterns. Our ego becomes locked in the mechanics of control patterns, and we will say, act, and react in ways that further fuel these control patterns; often times unconsciously. What may seem like unchecked, spoiled behavior in childhood, like grocery store tantrums, could translate later in life to addictive personalities or anger management issues.

Anger

Consider the metaphor that happiness is a starry sky on a clear night and the ego and control patterns are the clouds that obscure our clear views, often joined by emotions they foster: Anger, jealousy, fear and anxiety. Yet if we understand that our inner-self, like stars at night, is constant and unchanging, we can understand that the clouds that sometimes obscure them are temporary. The clouds can bring storms, even violent and turbulent tempests, but we know clouds pass, and our storms of emotions like anger can pass too.

In most cases, anger is met with anger. When someone angers you, your first response is usually to strike back as a way of protecting yourself from this combative situation. Once the ego is involved, there is a social pressure to return someone's anger with a measured response. Whether we yell or plot revenge, there is no proactive solution when we act in pure anger. Anger is a useless emotion that only muddles and confuses the mind. When you are boiled over in anger, constructive thought is absent. Anger can also intensify and even consume your peace and tranquility. It can close you off from situations entirely. Anger can create the darkest clouds that obscure the True Nature of your mind. Ironically, when your mind is full of anger, it is you, not your target, who suffers most. Be mindful of this.

Passive Fear

Coupled with ego and low self-esteem, fear is a disability, and is probably one of the most debilitating forms of suffering. Fear is a basic survival instinct that initiates a "fight, flight, or freeze" response. Pain or a threat of danger most often initiates a fear response. Fear allows us to recognize threats and react instinctively in order to survive. In survival situations, fear is useful. We should fear bears while hiking in forests and sharks while swimming in the ocean. Fight or flight is an instinctual part of our nature.

In situations that are not life or death – that are, for example, just life—fear becomes grouped with sets of smaller instinctual emotions like anger, sadness, and even exhilaration and joy. Fear is often also connected to the emotional state of anxiety. Anxiety, however, typically occurs without any immediate external threat, yet can freeze us into inaction. In situations where we don't literally have to fight to live, our fears often become anxieties. Fear becomes less of a quick call to action and more of a sustained dread. We fear losing our jobs, loneliness, or starting our own business.

A very common denominator to most fears in society is fear of failure and the fear of death. Societal fears, unlike fight or flight, are based on a conditioned or nurtured sense. Depending on how we were raised, on our sense of approval or disapproval from others, and our ego and self-esteem, we create a level of anxiety in ourselves that eats away at us as it builds.

The Responsive Universe

Countless studies show that stress alone is a major factor in high blood pressure, heart ailments, and disease, not to mention emotional instability and depression. Xanax is one of the most prescribed drugs in America. Guess what it treats? That's right, anxiety. In our daily lives where fight or flight typically means success or failure more than life or death, fear, stress and anxiety go hand in hand.

In order to combat these fears, we must recognize the truth of the First Mandala. Just as we cannot base our happiness and self-worth on money or possessions that are not guaranteed or constant, we cannot live focusing on our suffering. Suffering is not intrinsic to our existence. Much like the storm clouds that obscure our vision of the stars, suffering—more specifically, ego, anger, low self-esteem, and fear—are merely the factors that blur our vision of our True Nature (an energy source we will discuss shortly).

Our True Nature is the part of us that is guaranteed, constant, and pure. Connecting to True Nature and feeling free of stress, anxiety and fear is a form of space. Space gives rise to well being. When we suffer and feel stress or anger, we feel closed off in our minds. We feel hemmed in and weighed down by pressure as anxieties take hold. Have you ever gone on vacation and magically felt open and alive as you took a break from life to relax on a beach? The truth of the First Mandala is that True Nature is a spacious vision to which we can all connect. When you achieve the space, the distance from stress, the clear vision of your starry night sky, you have the ability to better handle fear. When you have space, you have more tolerance for all challenges that surround you.

Suffering

It seems that much in life centers on one simple word, suffering: An unsophisticated word, but a very complicated concept. Suffering appears to be intrinsic to humans at first glance: At birth we suffer, and during life we tend to suffer. The premise of a Responsive Universe is to limit the suffering that appears to be inherent to our existence here on Earth. Many times suffering is created by our own devices. We may be led to think that much of our suffering is out of our control. Ailments like disease and stress are examples of suffering that appear to live outside of our immediate power. Ironically, this is how our eyes see the planet when living in the "material world." The material world is a place filled with reactions, a place where we typically place blame and fault on exterior environments and very little energy is placed on our own internal devices. We as people are malleable like soft metal or clay. Our experiences in life mold us to act and react in a specific conditioned way. We react through ego-driven processes born from social evolution. We react to the chaos and clutter that closes off our personal spaces in life. We are always fighting to keep our head above the water. Sometimes we feel hemmed in, alone and confused, only able to react to all the challenges that come our way; unable to fully grasp happiness or our intended evolutionary path. The result is suffering in every facet imaginable. When one lives this way from birth to adulthood, we don't really think of it as suffering. We simply think that this is life and that there are no choices but what is handed to us through fate and luck. Further, the quality of life we see is based on what surrounds us—people, television, and celebrities tend to set the standard and again we react as a common culture to meet the perceived needs of others—rarely meeting our own needs.

Still, there is another path in life. It is a path less trodden on a road that is frequently uphill. It is sometimes difficult to walk uphill, especially when everyone around you is walking downhill—much as it is always easier to walk with the wind against your back instead of against your face. You may be asking yourself, "Why would I want to walk uphill if I can always walk downhill?" The answer is very simple: When you look at your life and even the planet as a whole—are people genuinely happy or is there a lot of suffering? Is religion really working or does it create more problems on a global scale? Why do we see pictures and stories of famine, holy war, and persecution on the news at night? Do you wish you could be happier? These questions are born out of the "material world"—the world where everyone is walking downhill because it is easier.

As you probably already know, anything good in life requires a little hard work. Once you can recondition your mind to live in a Responsive Universe, eventually you will not even experience your actions as walking uphill. Much as exercise conditions us to be stronger and more agile, living in a Responsive Universe will condition you to be more mindful and aware—your complete perspective in life will change and there will be a shift in what a "material world" reality is and what your "True Reality" is. This is called self-evolution. Further, the truths of the Universe will unfold as you realize your place in this magnificent creation that is the Cosmos—A vast realm rich with positive energy all of which is readily available if our intentions are genuine. How do we connect to this positive energy? True Nature…

True Nature

The opposite of the ego is our True Nature. At birth, our True Nature exists from indestructible energy—consciousness its new vehicle, an unyielding life source that for many is unfortunately obscured by the ego faculties born from societal immersion. The concept of True Nature is the intrinsic, immortal potential for reaching enlightenment that exists within the mind of every sentient being. Its source and energy are born from the Cosmos. True Nature is your transcendent link to the Universe. Based on quantum physics, matter and energy are connected at the sub-atomic level. You and I are an intrinsic part of this connection as is every living organism and all matter, tangible and intangible. The gift of humanity is our conscious ability to connect to this instinctual energy and understand that we are a part of its grand design. This is truly a rare gift.

Quantum mechanics is the study of matter and energy, proposing the revolutionary idea that energy is absorbed and released in minute quantities, and that all matter displays both wave-like and particle-like properties, especially when viewed at subatomic levels. Quantum mechanics suggests that the behavior of matter and energy is interconnected and that the effect of the observer on the physical system being observed at this level must be understood as a part of that system. As proven in the laboratory, just the act of observing elementary particles at the sub-atomic level changes their characteristics simply through the examination process. Through the act of observing matter in its smallest form, we may conclude that our own energy, conscious thoughts, and possibly even our DNA cellular structure interact with matter within our surroundings and beyond our surroundings. The connections could be infinite! Yes, our conscious energy is shifting and changing the fabric of the Universe before our eyes.

Do you understand the significance of this? This literally means that through our own actions and thoughts we are the forefront of creation. At the sub-atomic level our energy interacts with our environment, changing it for the better or for the worst. We can no longer consider ourselves and our lives as simply a blink of an eye in the history of time; or an atheistic anomaly. Science proves we are more than that.... We also can no longer consider ourselves under the omnipresent rule of a God that controls our fate and destiny. Instead, we are at the forefront of creation; we are the creators, humans themselves wielding the power of God through our own actions and reactions. We create heaven and we create hell. The essence of True Nature is the vehicle that connects human consciousness with the energy of the Universe. Really it is all one and the same: A system of order that governs all that exists.

Quantum energy, self-actualization and karma are all connected as one – the common denominator: Your True Nature!

Do you have a hard time believing that we are connected to everything in this proverbial tapestry of quantum energy, light, and instinctual wisdom? Just look around you… Look at the world we have created… Much at the hands of humans? It makes you wonder, doesn't it? We see this connection through scientific experiments and we see the same dynamism through prayer, karma, and healing energy. We also see the suffering on a global scale at the hands of greed and power. We are connected to this negatively, as well. It is inescapable. The proof is in the experience! It is so simple and yet humans are just now seeing the alchemy of our actions and reactions: That we are connected to this vast and impressive Responsive Universe. We are just now finally seeing the connection: The beauty that is our place, the power and energy we unknowingly wield. We are more special than we know, yet many of us ignore such revelations settling for blind faith and negativity. Yes, we can create our destiny. The problem that arises is that the ego and our false-self warps our vision of what we truly want and need in life. The result is normally something short of authentic. It is then that our thirst to awaken is dulled and we are dragged back into the world we have defined. Yet, that is exactly what we need to do! We need to awaken to our full potential. We need to awaken and connect to this illusive True Nature that exists within all sentient beings—something the mystics and those who are enlightened have known for thousands of years—our connection to the sublime...

Still, we need to be mindful that our own guilt and negativity might be keeping us from the gifts we are destined for.... Sometimes when you put too much thought into something it can have a reverse effect and prevent something authentic from flowering—especially if your fears and inhibitions are woven into a particular manifestation. In this, mindfulness is our best friend. Through space and awareness, through compassion, wisdom, and love, the correct path exists and will be illuminated when we finally let go of the dogmatic trappings that hold us prisoner. Every thought can matter; every action can have a consequence. Small shifts in our thought processes and actions may seem insignificant but over time, much like compound interest; our positivity will outshine negativity.

Now, ask yourself this: Do you want to live in a mediocre world with no control over your destiny or do you want to live in a Responsive Universe where creation and energy are within your grasp?

God defined by the Universe is conscious or responsive energy and therefore humans are also part of this dynamic, connected as one in a vast matrix of light and matter with a dash of instinctual consciousness that transcends earthly dogma. That is the definition of a Responsive Universe; where science explains energy healing and the power of prayer; where energy and love marry and allow us to evolve. Knowing this, we understand that religious dogma, the ego, and other social trappings are not representative of our true-self—they are merely distortions fed by the "material world."

Author's Note: *When I use the name "God," I do not refer to a deity in the form of a man. As I discuss in the Third and Fourth Mandalas, I refer to God as it relates to the Universe. God is an intelligible sphere of instinctual energy that is connected to everything. God, like the Universe, is everything that exists.*

True Nature is like the stars we see on a clear night. Stars seem to shift based on the Earth's rotations and seasons, but in North America, you will always see Orion in the winter sky and Andromeda in the summer sky. You can depend on seeing these constellations—even if you can't explain their genesis, they exist and have existed for millions of years. Our True Nature is also unchanging and a continual source of our energy. It is something you can always depend on. But, just as clouds obscure our vision of the stars on a stormy night, our egos obstruct our pathway to True Nature. The ego can cloud our judgment and create suffering.

In order to connect to this True Nature our thoughts need to be completely centered in the present; beyond fear and fantasy, past and future. It is not about the past—that is gone... It is not about the future—that has yet to arrive... it is about what is going on right now... and now... and now... Eighty percent of all your thoughts today were most likely replays of the past and day-dreaming about the future; focusing on fear and fantasy... These thoughts may bring some form of instant gratification, but they can also bring anxiety, dread, and a cluttered mind. Almost everything that is not in the present moment is ego-driven—your false-self. When you center yourself in the present or on a specific task like reading this book the moment at hand is more authentic. The present moment is a magical gap between the past and future, a reprieve from mediocrity, apprehension, and self-gratifying desire. Within those authentic gaps between thoughts is this amazing connection to energy, relaxation, reverence, and bliss. It is here in the present that thoughts slow, inspiration and awareness are fine-tuned, and there is this heartfelt feeling that we are evolving in the right direction. This is where you will connect to your True Nature, and it is here in the present that your heart wish or inner voice will speak. Your inner voice is your egoless instinct; your "true-self" that speaks wisdom and reveals an illuminated path to enlightenment. We all have this inner voice but the problem is that our egos voice tends to be louder. All those endless thoughts that are awash in your mind drown out the inner voice within. It is your inner voice that will guide you into the future soundly and confidently. This does not come easy but the more mindful you are, the more you will slowly shift into this grand and welcoming Responsive Universe. Over time your mind will train itself to live in a Responsive Universe and then things like meditation and mindfulness will become second nature—much like breathing in and out. By centering your thoughts in the present, you are creating space within the mind where wisdom and energy can arise.

True Reality

Living with an open mind allows us to question what we learned when we were young and impressionable. It allows us to challenge old ideas and ideals in order to reevaluate our belief systems, to make sure they are not prey to the lures of money and manipulation. Somewhere before and during adolescence, our egos are born and stabilized, these unconscious masters of false perception. An unchecked ego can become stuck in control patterns: Coping and behavioral mechanisms that can foster negativity in many forms. Control patterns can bring us anger, anxiety, and fear. They cause us to suffer and obscure our true realities.

Many of us lack a genuine level of self-esteem. Instead, we tend to be walking boutiques of bad habits and addictions. We gain our confidence through money, materialism, and self-gratification. We stumble through the day stressed out, confused, and empty. This is the reality that many of us live. Many of us even live it unknowingly. We think that is all there is to life.

Your "True Reality" is a notion that only you can define for yourself, as you alone can fully understand your purpose on Earth. To define your "True Reality," you need to let your mind drop away from what you have already perceived as reality. It is not something that happens instantly. It is a graduated process of development. In order to find our "True Reality," we must acknowledge our egos and what control patterns we have let govern our lives. We must evaluate our fears and our suffering and how they relate to our false perceptions of life. We must shift our consciousness to the present.

As mentioned, most of our aimless yet destructive thoughts come from feelings ingrained in either the past or the future. Thoughts anchored to our fantasy and fears are all interwoven into our false-self. To be more mindful of the present, we must tune out other people's voices, what happened at work the other day, materialistic urges, childhood memories, old teachers, family, television—virtually everything besides our own internal voices—to feel ourselves breathing and reaching out to the world with a true mind and heart. We must go on a journey of pure thinking and begin the journey with a fresh palate that we have wiped clean and can now color with our own perceptions and theories. Living in the moment brings us to a self that is pure and unfettered. It brings us closer to our True Nature.

When we connect to our True Nature, we connect to something permanent and indestructible, something that can never be taken from us, and in this, we foster a bond that cannot be destroyed. Through this bond, we are free to connect to "True Reality," the higher level of sensitivity that transcends all things earthly. When we understand that we can attain this power and that it is already within us, unchanged and undestroyed, we can make better, self-directed decisions in life. This is a confidence that cannot be shaken by social pressures or ego. This is a confidence that is steadfast and indestructible. By clearing the pathways to our True Nature, we abandon fear and negativity—we achieve a higher level of illumination.

The First Mandala

Control patterns born from previous experiences can foster negativity in many forms. Somewhere before and during adolescence, our ego is formed, the unconscious master of false perception. An unchecked ego breeds many forged emotions like anger, jealousy, and fear. Often unaware of our inner plight, we continue down our path of fear and low self-esteem, and we suffer. Our fear and suffering are directly related to our false perceptions of life. Living with an open mind allows us to question what has been presented to us when we were young and impressionable. It allows us to challenge old ideals and control patterns to better evaluate our belief systems to confirm that they were not founded due to negative outside influences. It opens us up to understanding True Nature as a pure and unwavering source of happiness. We have the sovereign power to embrace our own thoughts and convictions. Living with an open mind, being receptive to change, and having a willingness to work for it are the first steps toward liberation.

First Mandala Exit Summary

- Live with an open mind.
- Embrace mindfulness in daily life—this includes thoughts, emotions and your surroundings.
- Revisit old belief systems and redefine their significance as it relates to you presently.
- Understand the concept of True Nature and that it is pure and unwavering.
- Acknowledge your ego and control patterns and how it obscures your "True Reality."
- Understand that fear and suffering is related to a false perception of life.

The Second Mandala

The Art of Meditation

Spaciousness

Recall that the reality of the First Mandala is that True Nature is a spacious vision to which we can all connect; an indestructible and boundless life force present within all conscious beings. Space is the quality of openness in our minds. Imagine the space it takes to hold the countless thoughts that race through our heads each day. Imagine the space it takes to hold memories, dreams, skills, and lessons. Physically, the brain seems small, but the mind appears to be vast, maybe infinite. In the First Mandala, we compared our spacious minds to a clear night, a starry sky, free from the clouds of stress and fear. In the Second Mandala, we will take this analogy even further. Visualize True Nature again as the endless night sky. The stars we see at night are actually neighborhood stars that are just a handful of the billions of stars within our Milky Way Galaxy. Now imagine a Universe with billions of galaxies each home to billions more stars. The Cosmos is vast, maybe infinite.

Much like the Cosmos, our True Nature is also vast and seemingly infinite. In fact, once you connect to your True Nature, there is a feeling that the mind and the Universe are connected. There are billions of atoms within the human brain alone; each akin to its own unique vibration and the collective vibration of the Universe. We are all connected in a vast symphony of sub atomic energy. The immensity of the Universe boggles the mind, and the spacious nature of the human brain amazes and mystifies us as well. While you can measure a human brain for size and depth, when you think of the mind and all its processes and capabilities, it seems to defy dimensions and appears infinite.

In the era when common belief was that the Earth was flat, ancient thinkers believed that when you looked up at the night sky, what you saw was the extent of all that existed. This sort of thinking—that the world only consists of thoughts and things within your own tangible realm of perception—is what breeds close-minded and primitive observations of life. These kinds of observations can lead to ignorance, stress, fear, anxiety, exclusivity, and hate. Imagine trying to count every grain of sand on Earth. It is impossible, right? Even though it is impossible to count every grain, you know that a vast quantity of other grains exists on beaches that you can't even see.

*In early meditative practice, the key is to connect
to the quality of space as it relates to the mind*

Primitive thinkers found this notion unsettling—that more existed beyond which they could perceive. Yet, there is actually comfort in trusting that our world and True Nature are spacious. The Universe just exists, and there is nothing we need to do to make it exist. Many times in life, we feel there is little we can count on. Home prices and the stock market fluctuate. Love and friendship can be fleeting. We age and eventually die. One thing is constant and unchanging: The spacious vision of True Nature that exists within us all. Our minds, like the Universe, are vast and boundless realms where countless things are possible. There is space for everything in our lives because the Universe and the human mind has unending space.

The Art of Meditation

The art of meditation is a lifestyle tool that helps calm the mind and allows for the quality of endless space to arise from within. It is from this space that clarity and awareness wells (the essence of mindfulness). Meditation allows us to slow and impede the incessant thoughts that ripple through our consciousness and find that inner realm that resides just below the surface of our ego. There is a shift in perspective and mindfulness that leaves the static of this "material world" we live in behind and thus allows us to embark on a journey inward and outward all in the same breath—thus connecting to our True Nature. There are no boundaries when we discuss the concept of True Nature, much as there are no boundaries within this vast Cosmos that is everything. All that is matter and energy has no edge or periphery. When we consider the mind again, the same notion seems to hold true. Just as we can quantify the vastness of our Universe, we can easily quantify our brain as being something small and tangible. Yet when we think about thoughts, dreams and memories, how large is the mind? What constitutes a thought and where does it come from? Where does it go? When you contemplate the mind, can you see boundaries? Is it fixed and condensed, or spacious and unending? It makes you wonder, doesn't it?

These are questions worth pondering, because once you connect to the idea of space and how it relates to our minds, our True Nature, and the Universe, you may come to the realization that there are no boundaries and that literally anything is possible. Once we can connect to the concept of space, the world around you will become larger and more maneuverable. Simple, crude emotions like anger, jealousy, and even fear will seem less ominous and controlling. With this new spacious mindset, there will be room for the challenges that face us each day. Imagine a world with less stress, conflict, and anxiety. Connecting to the concept of spaciousness is the gateway to a Responsive Universe: Vast, interconnected, and pulsing with positive quantum energy.

So how does one connect to this quality of openness? Well, it begins with meditation. There are many forms of meditation including traditional or formal meditation. Most of my techniques are derived from the Dzogchen tradition of Tibetan Buddhism. Still, over the years, I have fine-tuned my practice to meet my personal needs. Eventually you will do the same. We will discuss formal meditation at a later time, but for now it is worth mentioning a much more approachable path to meditation that I call "daily life practice."

The concept of daily life practice is simply an extension of the meditative process. Its core focus is simply mindfulness. It is a process of being aware and more attentive of the present. As we have discussed, when we stop and focus on the endless parade of thoughts in our mind we come to realize that most of these impulses of energy are rooted in the past or future. When we remain rooted in the past and future, our mental processes are governed by the ego: Emotions and feelings of anger, fear, jealousy, guilt and fantasy. Rarely are we connected with the moment which is pure and unfettered; the pathway to your True Nature. One repeatable exercise is to ask yourself the following question: How do I feel right now? Do you feel positive, negative, or just neutral? By asking this question, you are connecting to the present and thus side-stepping the ego momentarily. Taste the thoughts that follow: Are they rooted in the future or past? For a couple moments label your thoughts as guests as they enter the mind. Treat each thought equally and then let it dissolve away as the next thought arises. Can you put your finger on where your thoughts entered the mind and where they exited? Did they exit? The concept of meditation is not about stopping your thoughts from forming. There is this misconception with meditation that one needs to clear the mind of all thoughts—I can tell you this is virtually impossible. Meditation is about the thoughts that come and go in our minds. The first step in meditation is to simply be aware of all the thoughts. This is a concept that should not be reserved specifically for meditation but folded into a daily life practice.

Another simple exercise in mindfulness is being aware of your breathing. Something as simple as the "in and out" of breath is an example of being rooted in the present. For a few moments, breathe slowly and deeply into your abdomen pushing your diaphragm down into your stomach or belly. Try to hold a deep breath in for couple of seconds and then slowly release the air and any notions of stress or negativity. Do this several times being aware of the "in and out" of your inhalation. Feel the warm and cool sensations of simple mindful breathing. At the same time, label any thoughts that enter your mind as guests. It is the breath that connects the body with the mind. After several deep breaths, ask yourself how do you feel: Do you feel positive, negative, or neutral? Was there any shift in feeling or emotion? Are you amazed by all the thoughts that traverse the mind in such a short time? Maybe try this process again later in the day: Breathe in and breathe out; then be mindful of your constant streaming of thoughts. Do you feel good, bad, or just neutral? This simple technique is an example of mindfulness, which is in essence meditation and can be used throughout the day as a daily life practice. Such exercises allow us to stop, pause, and take a break from the static and controlled chaos that surrounds us. It allows us to be aware of our thoughts and emotions in the now—if only momentarily. Being present in the moment is an important facet of emotional stability and happiness. The more you are rooted in the present, the more space and clarity will be actualized.

The first lesson or objective above was to become more aware of your thoughts, label them as guests, and be more mindful of the present. Seems easy enough, right? If you are reading this book, then there is a pretty good chance you have tried meditation before. I can certainly recall my first meditation attempts: A train wreck is probably the best description. One would think finding time to self-actualize would be the most difficult facet of meditation. With such busy lives, when can we find time to meditate? Others may think that the most difficult part of meditation is sitting in one spot for an extended period of time. Truthfully, the most challenging part of meditation is fielding all the thoughts that parade through our heads at any given point. Sure your first meditation seems to start off well: You feel mindful and are focused on your out-breath (at least for a few seconds). Then almost unknowingly, bizarre thoughts enter your mind: The Festivus episode on Seinfeld. Do dogs have feelings? What happened to the peanuts they used to serve on airplanes? Did I leave the refrigerator door ajar? Before you know it you are completely side-tracked and the first instinct for most of us is to get frustrated.

There lies the second lesson in meditation: Do not get frustrated when your mind gets side-tracked. Why should our thoughts frustrate us? Thoughts are thoughts and there is no reason to get frustrated. All frustration does is erode the peace in our minds—completely the opposite of what we are trying to do here. I talked earlier about being more mindful of the present. As we now realize, most of our egos facilities function in the past and future: Feeding off our unorganized thoughts of fear and fantasy. When we are rooted in the present, we are a part of life in the now, connected, unfettered, and alive. Still, even when our minds are rooted in the present, it is impossible to stop the incessant thoughts that careen through our heads at any given moment—this is simply how the mind operates. But we do have control over how we manage these thoughts. Again, a good approach is to simply label your thoughts as guests. A thought will materialize; you will process it as a guest in your mind, and then let it dissolve into nothingness. Instead of being focused on the content of the thought, think of where the thought came from and where it is going. As the thought dissolves, refocus your attention on the present. Focusing on the "in and out" breath is the best tactic for staying mindful of the present. To reiterate, rhythmic breathing connects the mind with the body and focusing on your breath is crucial to successful meditation. I will talk more about this later.

As a novice (during meditation) you may have to retrain or re-focus the mind a 100 times or more during a 20-minute meditation session. This can be mentally exhaustive and may seem unproductive. Yet, there is a completion of the process. You see, the mind is like any other muscle in the human body. The more you use it the stronger and more fit it becomes. Many of us live life on the edge of controlled disarray—our lives are wrought with stress, drama, and even anxiety. This is because we let our egos govern our thoughts and actions. Much like the laws of karma, what we put out in the Universe will return to us as an equal response or level of energy. When our mind is not at peace, we are not at peace. Meditation is about acknowledging all the thoughts in our heads as guests and then immediately shifting our focus back to the present. Again, meditation focuses on centering your attention on the present (connecting to the out-breath) and continually refocusing every time your mind strays from the present and your rhythmic breathing. It will take time, but eventually all those incessant thoughts will calm and simply be a backdrop to more productive meditative thoughts. Further, repetition is the key to success. Even if you feel you are not benefiting from meditation, keep at it and do not give up. Your mind is growing stronger and more stable with each new session. It is the constant push and pull of refocusing your thoughts when you get side-tracked that builds stability and thus a successful practice. Think of meditation as being similar to lifting weights. Each repetition is an example of refocusing your mind on the present. Eventually your mind will be a skilled and sharpened tool of mindfulness. Also, extend your breathing and mindfulness into your daily life and over time shift your entire perspective away from ego, past, and future, and into the present.

There are three areas or facets of meditation:

- **Set and Focus**
- **Deepening and Appreciation**
- **Exit and Daily Life Practice**

To begin any meditation, you need to set aside a time when there will be the least amount of distraction. Any amount of time is acceptable for meditating. A longer session (30-60 minutes) is ideal, but even five minutes a day is better than not meditating at all. Busy lives always present unforeseen challenges that make it difficult to find a time, so carving out a consistent time slot in your schedule just dedicated to meditation is often best. I have personally found that the best time to meditate is early in the morning right after waking up. The mind is calm and still in a sedated state. As the day wears on, our minds become inundated with thoughts, concerns, fears, and fantasies that make meditation a little more challenging. Still, many find a meditation session before bedtime peaceful and therapeutic. As you settle into a regular practice, soon you will find a time that is better suited to your lifestyle. There is no wrong or right time to meditate. The key is making time to meditate and sticking to the regiment.

You can meditate almost anywhere. The most successful and deep meditations occur when you are stationary and in a seated position. Many practitioners suggest sitting upright with legs crossed in the lotus position with your hands and arms relaxed and outward on your legs. I encourage you to find any comfortable seated position. It can include a chair or couch with a comfortable back. The objective is to feel comfortable so you do not feel confined or fidgety and are able to focus on your inner-self. If you find a chair more comfortable than the lotus position then I recommend placing your feet flat on the floor to feel grounded and stable. However if you are most comfortable in a formal seated posture as is seen in statues of a meditating Buddha, allow your arms to fall relaxed onto your legs with your hands outstretched and open. This type of posture is symbolic to quantum energy—free and flowing—and the openness demonstrates that you have no fear, or at least do not let fear dictate your actions and feelings. Comfortable and relaxed, with arms outstretched and hands open; you are now ready to attract positive energy and proactive thoughts.

Learning to meditate and being diligent with your practice is an important step to achieving self-actualization

As you sit, even if aided by a chair, try to keep your spine straight. This will help you stay alert and will also help you avoid falling asleep. I suggest closing your eyes at first to avoid distraction from your immediate surroundings. As you become more skilled in your meditation practice, it is fine to meditate with eyes open—in fact many prefer it (assuming there are no visual elements like a television to distract your attention).

Now that you are physically "set," it is time to "focus" on beginning a meditation session. The meditative focus is not clearing our thoughts from the mind; the focus is on the thoughts that come and go in our minds. Thoughts naturally occur and are a fundamental action of the mind. It is virtually impossible to stop the process. The art of meditation is to slow thoughts and lengthen the gap between them so that our mind is not awash with chaos, stress, and anxiety. Meditation is about finding the space between thoughts and focusing on its peace and wisdom.

Start with a rhythmic breathing pattern. If you are feeling a little stressed or silly about meditating for the first time, relax and remember that people have been meditating for thousands of years. Breathe slowly and deeply into your abdomen, pushing your diaphragm down into your stomach. Try to

The Responsive Universe

hold a deep breath for a moment and then slowly release the air out, also releasing stress and negative feelings. Continue this until you feel comfortable breathing in a more usual pattern. Your mental focus should be entirely on your breathing patterns. You should feel more relaxed and grounded after this. The breath connects the body to the mind. Inhale and feel the weight of the air in your lungs. Exhale and feel all the stress and weight leave you.

It may be helpful to say "in" as you breathe in and "out" as you breathe out. Use this as your mantra for the first exercise. A mantra is a word or group of words that can assist in keeping your mind focused on the moment. As you continue to breathe in and out, you will most likely notice random thoughts that come and go. You may experience feelings, both pleasant and unpleasant. Just simply notice them and allow them to pass along. Refocus on your new mantra, "in...out," and treat every thought and feeling that enters your mind the same—as if they were just guests traveling through space and time. Continue to do this for at least twenty minutes. It is always fine to return to the breathing pattern if your mind wanders away too far. Above all, just relax and settle into the experience, whatever it may be.

Fight the urge to get up or quit. During your meditation, you may feel that the endless thoughts and lack of focus is a sign of a failed session. This is not true as there is no such thing as a failed session. Any thoughts, feelings and emotions you sense are all part of the meditative experience—coupled with rhythmic breathing; meditation is any experience that unfolds before you. Just settle into the experience no matter the outcome or result. Thoughts will continue to bounce into your head one after another. This is totally normal. Simply just try to be mindful of the thought processes. Think of yourself as an observer with no real link or connection to the thoughts. You may have to refocus a hundred times or more during a twenty-minute session. Again, that is totally normal. An early meditation exercise that is helpful is to continue your breathing patterns, and as your thoughts race through your mind, visualize trying to grab the thoughts with your hands. As soon as you mentally grab a thought, it often disappears. Where did it go? This will get you back on track with your breathing and may also give you a glimpse of all the space that is in your mind. So much space for thoughts!

Another useful early meditation tool is to become mindful of your body and immediate surroundings. While still focusing on your breathing, direct your internal attention to your toes. Can you feel them? How do they feel? I know it sounds odd, but keep at it. While still focusing on your breath, work your way up your body. Visualize your legs and internally feel them. Is there pain or discomfort? Do they feel relaxed and at peace? Move up to your stomach and lungs, your shoulders and neck, your arms and fingers. Take your time and be open to the experience of being mindful of your body. Get in tune with your body and the internal feelings you may be sensing. Maybe you're hungry or you feel a small pain in your back. Maybe you can hear your own heartbeat, only it sounds like it's coming from your brain. Now, turn to your surroundings. Listen for creaks in the floor and birds outside. Start cataloguing all of your outward sensory perceptions. Please always remember to return to your breathing pattern. This exercise helps you to gain clarity and is an excellent way to begin a meditation, as it tends to calm and to sharpen the mind.

To aid in curbing thoughts about when your meditation will end or how long you've been at it, set a timer or a watch, though its alarm should be subtle and not jerk you abruptly from your session. You can also try guided or meditative music and use the end of a particular song as your signal to end your meditation. There are even special meditation timers and applications available for computers and smart phones that can assist in the meditative process. Even candles and incents can help to accent and heighten the meditative experience.

Your brain is like any other muscle in your body. The more you use it and exercise it, the stronger it becomes. Meditative exercises will strengthen your brain's capacity and stability. From the endless stream of thoughts, great clarity and structure will arise. The art of meditation will stretch those gaps between thoughts, allowing for a deeper world awareness to take hold. Even if you consider your first few meditations unsuccessful because you felt disturbed or had a lot on your mind, there is still much to be gained from any kind of meditative practice. It is important that you don't give up or decide that meditation is not a good tool for you. Over the course of time, meditation will strengthen and stabilize your mind and also give you a greater ability to control your moods and emotions.

Deepening and Appreciation

With any meditative session, you will begin with your set and focus to get comfortable and concentrate on your breathing. After achieving command of this phase of meditation, next comes a feeling of "deepening and appreciation." As you become more comfortable with your breathing patterns, they will become automatic, like a backdrop in your mind allowing a new lesson or thought to be your primary focus. Use a mantra to help with breathing and focus. Again, it is totally normal for your mind to wander as new thoughts or perspectives enter your mind. Just continue to treat all thoughts as guests, and when you feel like you've gotten sidetracked, gently refocus on your breathing. Never get frustrated by the many thoughts you have—just simply be aware of them and move on.

Over time, a deepening and appreciation within your heart and mind will emanate from your practice. You will eventually craft the ability to isolate social static, your ego, and the control patterns that shape you and connect more to your True Nature. The goal of meditation is to find your inner voice that speaks the truth and wants one thing only—happiness. Not happiness as it relates to the ego's needs, but happiness as it relates to True Nature. Through meditation, you will settle into a level of clarity and space that breeds an innate level of responsiveness. You will feel a new confidence that springs from a deeper level within yourself. It isn't a confidence that feeds a false or hollow self, but a confidence that wells up from deep within and brings a smile to your face for no apparent reason. It is a confidence that tells you that everything is going to be all right. It is True Nature speaking from the source—energy, wisdom, and love. It is from the silence in between thoughts that your self-discovery and insight wells. Like cracks or shards of light through bricks, illumination will find its way if you slow your thoughts and live in the present—if only for a moment. If you are new to meditation, be mindful that this is possible, that anything is indeed possible when you settle into the warmth and illumination of your True Nature.

The second step of deepening and appreciation is a continual work in progress. As you traverse through the Nine Mandalas, you will begin to find a new person. That new person is a self-actualized you! Deepening and appreciation will stem from your openness to self-discovery and gaining clarity and responsiveness from a fuller understanding of yourself. You will become more mindful of your thoughts, emotions and also the thoughts and emotions of others. You will begin to notice elements in nature and within your immediate surroundings that once seemed dull and uninteresting but now have a new luster and appeal. This is the beginning of your awakening and the gateway to this new-found paradise is through meditation.

Exit and Daily Life Awareness

The exit or completion of a meditative session should be relaxed and smooth. Slowly open your eyes if they were closed, and feel free to stretch while getting up from your meditative position. Pause and find reverence and gratitude for this new adventure in mindfulness you have disembarked on. Drink a glass of water to hydrate your body. Then, maybe take a moment to go outside and breathe in some fresh air. Focus on an element of nature—a cloud floating by, a tree, a flower, or just take in the view you see. Examine and appreciate the detail and the beauty in what you observe, and then go about your day.

This type of exercise is another example of daily life practice. Focusing on the detail in what you observe around you is a way to take your meditative sessions further into your daily activities. Daily life practice allows us to be more in control of our minds and more focused on the controlled chaos that often runs the day. After your first meditation, you will be aware of how busy and overactive the mind can be. Sure, you knew that your mind was always thinking, but have you ever tried to slow the thinking and examine all of the thoughts? Have you asked what a thought really is and where it comes from and where it goes when you stop thinking it? Reveling in the details of thoughts and observations will allow you to bridge the gap between your meditation practice and the day's activities. Increasing your level of awareness in both realms will enhance each experience and create a continual cycle of deepening and appreciation. Increased awareness breeds an increased sense of self.

Meditation Session

If you have not done so, go ahead and plan your first meditation session. Find a time that works best for you and try to limit the distractions. Again, it is fine to use music as an aid or gauge for time, as long as it is conducive to meditation and relaxation. Remember your posture and breathing. During this first session, really make breathing the focus. As thoughts enter your mind, treat them as guests and gently allow them to fade off into the spaciousness of your mind. Always try to refocus on your breathing as the mainstay of your meditative session and all future sessions. Use your first mantra: "In" as you breathe in and "out" as you breathe out. Repeat this mantra every time your mind strays so that you can return to rhythmic breathing. Do not get frustrated if all your expectations were not met. Simply do your best, and that is enough.

"If you are new to practice it's important to realize that simply to sit on that cushion for fifteen minutes is a victory".

Charlotte Joko Beck

Try to be more mindful of your body during your first session. Once your breathing is moving at a nice rhythmic pace, start at your toes and mentally visualize your body from heels to head and in between—visualize from fingers to spine, from stomach to brain. Settle into this new mindfulness of your body. Listen and become aware of your own vessel of life.

Keep your first session light. Your first several sessions will be battles of patience and varying levels of frustration. The point of your first meditation is to complete the session and nothing more. As you will find, it is challenging enough to sit in one place and just focus inward. Five minutes may seem like an eternity.

After you meditate, review the daily life practice exercise that follows. It is best to continue your meditation and daily life practice throughout the course of three to five days. Meditate on one single thought or guided exercise for several days so that you make an effective mental imprint. It takes the human brain up to seven attempts to fully memorize something. Meditating on the same thought or concept over the course of several sessions will allow your mind to generate new inspirations and insight. Now go and try your new meditation practice and settle into the notion that you are working to self-evolve beyond just the ordinary.

Daily Life Practice

The purpose of this exercise is to make you more aware of what is going on inside your head. After your first meditation, think about all the thoughts that flowed through your mind. Did you find your mind wandering from your focus on breathing? For most people, the answer is yes. There is nothing wrong with your mind wandering. It is a natural process that happens all day long. Even while we dream at night, the mind wanders from one dream to another. We go through our days with thousands of thoughts streaming in our head without really noticing any of them. This stream of thoughts is called mental chatter. If you take notice of your mental chatter, you will see that many of the thoughts coming and going are rooted in fear and the past and in fantasy and future.

Be aware of your constant stream of thinking and on occasion, pause and take notice of what you are thinking. Are your thoughts positive, negative, or neutral? What are you feeling as you take notice of what you're thinking? As you become more aware of your mental chatter, greet your thoughts differently as you continue to try to focus on your breathing during your meditations and daily life practice. Spend a couple seconds with your thoughts as they wander in and then gently guide them out as you refocus on your breath. Acknowledge the frustration you may feel as your mind wanders as a trigger of new awareness of your mind. Try to find some amusement in your thoughts. You may be surprised at what pops up in your head and your mind's immediate shift to something new and completely unrelated. If your first few meditative sessions felt like frothing seas of mental chatter with little organization and structure, then you had a successful session. This is how the mind works, and most of the time we are oblivious to our mind's content and functions. The purpose of your early meditations and this daily life practice is to become an observer and nothing more.

Make it a practice as each day progresses to continue to pay attention to the thoughts that flow through your mind. It is especially helpful to do this exercise when your mind is free to think of anything, say, when you are walking the dog, commuting somewhere, or doing a similar activity where there is no major mental task at hand. The point is not to make this awareness a burden—the idea is just to pause on occasion and become aware of mental chatter at any point during the day and greet these thoughts as guests moving through your mind. Then refocus on something you observe in nature for only a moment—perhaps the sky, a cloud, a tree, or even a break from your computer screen at work to gaze out the window. Take a deep breath and then continue your day. Breathe in, breathe out, and move on.

This exercise can be successful on many levels. Even if you find it exhausting to continue to refocus your thoughts, at least you are becoming more aware of what is going on in your mind. Eventually, you will achieve a genuine level of clarity. You will feel sharper. Your thoughts will be more vivid. Soon, inspirations may strike, and you may feel more positive about life for no apparent reason. Continue to be more and more aware of your responses to things. Take note of positive, negative, and neutral responses. After a few days of this practice, you will feel more mindful of your body and immediate surroundings. Soon the practice will become second nature like breathing.

The Second Mandala

The truth of the First Mandala is that True Nature is a spacious vision to which we can all connect. The truth of the Second Mandala is that this concept of spaciousness exists not only in the Universe, but also within our minds. Spaciousness is best defined as being open. It is true stability in any situation in life. Having an open mind is crucial to self-discovery, and being open to change means creating space for all experiences without allowing our reactions to govern them.

We make space and open ourselves up to the infinite vision of True Nature through devices like meditation and daily life practice. The devices show us that under all the ego and co-dependency that seems like reality, there is a constant, unwavering force we can all depend on that is as spacious as it is endless. Allowing spaciousness to enter our minds and lives gives us the ability to face all of life's challenges and make good decisions. The brain may seem small physically, but the mind is vast. If we connect to this space, gone will be stress and anxiety. We will have infinite space for clarity and truth. Incorporate meditation into your daily life and you will see a different world reveal itself to you—a "True Reality" beyond ego and false-self.

Second Mandala Exit Strategy

- Understand the qualities of space—a boundless attribute of the mind.
- Find faith and permanence in your unwavering True Nature.
- Find time for meditation.
- Meditate on inner self; focus on breathing and continue to label your thoughts as guests. Be mindful of the present.
- Mantra: "Breathe in, breathe out."
- Daily Life Practice: Treat your thoughts as guests and be internally and externally mindful.

The Third Mandala

Religion, God, Creation and the Universe

Religion

Recall that True Nature is a spacious vision of the Universe to which we can all connect. Once we experience an awakening and connect to our True Nature, we are linked to the Universe, this amazing tapestry of nature, love, and energy. Even though we can't fully explain what the Universe is and how it came to be, we sense its awesomeness and our part in the puzzle. The Universe made us, yet we can't fully define it. But we try. And we try to determine the purpose in our connection to it. Often theories about the creation of the Universe and our purpose in it are categorized as religious thinking.

I believe religion is one's sacred engagement with his or her spiritual reality. It is not an institute that is fixed, nor does it have clear boundaries. It is an aspect of the human experience that intersects, incorporates, and even transcends other aspects of life and society. Religion is meant to be a personal experience. Its meaning should be determined by individual spiritual needs.

Today, organized religion is interwoven into many aspects of our lives from politics to schooling. A man-made concept, organized religion has been a fundamental force in our social environment for thousands of years. Most religions offer moral guidelines by which followers strive to live. They also provide explanations of the world's creation and rewards of an afterlife or rebirth after a life lived saintly or sinfully.

Ancient Religion

From the beginning of humankind, various isolated societies have constructed religious belief systems based mostly on their prehistoric environments and subsistence strategies. Farmers of the ancient Middle East, for example, worshipped gods for fertility of the soil, availability of water, and the conversion of grain in food preparation. Shepherds and herders prayed to gods concerned with the fertility and safety of their sheep, goats, and cattle. In the marshlands of Babylonia, people considered fish and other river creatures sacred. Keepers of the orchards associated gods with the productivity of the date palm and its clusters of life-giving fruit. Ancient people also identified striking features of their environments, such as mountains and rivers, as gods. For example, the peninsula beside the Tigris River inspired the birth of Ashur, the ancient god of the Assyrians.

Modern Religion

As cultures matured and developed into modern societies, they revolutionized their religious belief systems. Modern religion turned religious thought from subsistence strategies and survival to thoughts of sins and redemption. This renaissance developed caste systems, karma, enlightenment, and the Four Noble Truths in the East. Western civilization saw the birth of Christ and the marriage of church and state. Ancient religions evolved over time due to education and increased self-awareness. Religious thought progressed along with culture, becoming more concerned with philosophy, politics, and promised roads to salvation.

Why are there so many religions? Asking that question is like asking why there are so many languages. Different cultures divided by geography and race will birth greatly diverse religious systems. Despite many differences among cultures, there is one striking similarity that all groups of people tend to share: A need for spirituality. Still, what inspires the mind to focus so much energy on a "Religious God," an invisible and, often times, unproven force? The Pillars of Religion briefly outline the major building blocks that support our thirst for theology in contemporary society.

The theoretical pillars are as follows:

Cause and Effect

Cultures developed religions thousands of years ago to answer specific cause and effect situations. Imagine this: The year is 180 B.C., and an indigenous tribe in equatorial Africa has faced three long years of parching drought conditions. They have no reasonable answer for the monumental crop loss and resulting famine in their villages. Many of the village elders attribute their loss and hunger to a punishment from the gods. We bring meaning to unavoidable or inexplicable experiences when we attribute them to divine will. In the primitive village, the elders call for prayers and sacrifices to atone for any wrongdoings that have angered their deities. Eventually rain will fall again and the drought will diminish, but the reprieve in suffering will only strengthen the faith of the villagers who see inexplicable events as acts of gods.

People still use religion as a tool to provide sound explanations for events that occur without any palpable reasons. When a "God-fearing" family loses a loved one, we often explain it in terms that comfort and satisfy them.

We rationalize the tragedy as an act of God: God has other plans for her, she is in a much better place, only God knows why he was taken at such a young age, and so forth. Explaining tragedies as God's plan brings comfort and closure to unthinkable situations.

Social Interaction

Humans are social animals. Many people rely on religion to give them a feeling of belonging to a group of society. History has even shown that often people who do not belong to mainstream religious movements become social outcasts: Social pressures and the attraction to being part of something larger and important in life helps fuel religion.

Imagine the pioneers who lived centuries ago on deserted plains across the Midwest. Life was difficult with daily rituals that revolved around work for survival. The pioneers lived in total isolation on large ranches and farms, miles from their closest neighbor. Riding into town for supplies or attending church was the highlight of their social lives. Even in present times, church is a friendly place to meet people, to sing, listen to music, and feel connected to others around you. Religious groups connect communities and bring people together, especially around holidays.

Crutch in Life

Many people unknowingly use religion as a crutch in life for many reasons—love, self-esteem, dependent and compulsive personality disorders, or as a band-aid for all of life's problems. Sigmund Freud believed religion was our primitive attempt to deal with the frightening realities of the world and the impossibility of satisfying our fundamental desires. In his view, religion was a response to fear and longing. He believed that love for and fear of the father found symbolic expression in major religious traditions.

Many people use religion as a guide through life in hopes that God will clear a path and reveal to them the way to self-actualization. Religion provides answers and direction for life's biggest concerns, woes, and wishes. An individual's religious faith is often as strong as the intensity of his or her worries and desires in life.

The Responsive Universe

Fear

Fear of death is another major component in the Pillars of Religion, more precisely, the fear of what comes after death. Do we face a black, soundless eternity devoid of all thought and feeling? Religions assure us that there is life after death. For some, life itself is an arduous journey of all work and no play and seeing many loved ones die before you. Believing there is a rebirth or an afterlife of peace and relaxation is a major aspect supporting religions interest. Religions bring many peace of mind with the ideas that hard work, suffering, and faith are the keys to a heavenly paradise.

The merger of church and state in the medieval era established an interesting phenomenon that carries into the present day as well. Religion was instrumental in keeping the poor majority from rising up against the wealthy church and state unions. Tyrannical monarchies backed by the church would promise salvation to the peasants who worked hard and lived in poverty, their only satisfaction being the reward of heaven. These peasants believed if they had faith, they would sit among the nobles in a blissful afterlife.

In modern times, the church still uses religion as a way to condition children and adults to adopt "good" behavior, often times using fear and guilt. The whole idea of sin is a meter for measuring bad behavior, and religious authorities are the ones who often determine what is "right or wrong" within a culture. We adopt Commandments and Noble Truths to illustrate the proper way for a good person to live his or her life. Threats of hell, promises of heaven, and edicts from guidebooks of morality like the Bible or Quran provide a framework for strong mental conditioning. You follow the rules in order to find your way to eternal paradise. Or, as in Hinduism, you must live many lives and undergo many positive experiences before you attain perfection and become one with divinity.

Need for Faith

The final and most important Pillar of Religion is our true need for spirituality. There is a distinct divide between faith and religion. Religion is a set of beliefs concerning the cause, nature, and purpose of the Universe. Religion cannot be proven right or wrong—it simply stands by itself, held up by the faith of its parishioners. Faith is the confidence and trust in a set of ideologies, not often based on fact or proof. To put it more simply, religion is a vehicle for human faith. Humans need faith to exist positively in an environment, especially a negative or seemingly helpless one. Prayer, after all, in this light is really just an exercise in positive thinking. Faith goes even further to instill an uplifting, empowering feeling in an individual. We cannot know for certain, for example, if Jesus rose from the dead or that heaven exists. We cannot peer into the future and see an afterlife of all-knowing peace. But we can have faith in it.

Religion and Self

How we came to be and where we go when we die are as monumental as topics come when pondering life's big quandaries. Because religious thinking often gives purpose and meaning to a sometimes cruel and indefinable world, it is hard to dive into religious discussions without insulting someone's beliefs in some way. People get defensive of their religious beliefs and often cannot take any criticism about them. Some protect their religious beliefs with an intensity that is fanatical and though I would not call it a benchmark, the more fanatical one is with their specific religious philosophy, the more deeply rooted fear they probably harbor. Being ridiculously defensive alludes to a weakness in thinking; whether it's because of ego, self-esteem, or ignorance, fanaticism points to a flaw in one's belief system.

As we discussed in the First Mandala, in order for self-discovery to take place, we need to strip down the layers in our thinking, of our childhood beliefs and ideals, to isolate their sources and determine if our thinking is unadulterated and genuine about who we are. Much like parents, mentors, and friends who influence us and contribute to how we think, religion is one of the biggest influences in our lives. Our religious upbringing colors our perspectives as children and adults to form the mindset on which we base our daily actions and decisions. In many cultures, religion is a social law and is embraced without question. Is this bad? Not necessarily. In many cases, religion does encourage us to live well and be kind and promote positive energy through prayer. It becomes troublesome, however, when religion manufactures control patterns in our lives and encourages the belief that a singular religious path is the only path of the righteous and worthy. That control pattern breeds only close-minded thinking and facilitates persecution and violence. We also see flaws in religion when its morals are influencing law, gender rights, and facilitating jihad or holy wars.

As we strip down the layers of our thinking to determine which beliefs are intrinsic to who we are, we find an interesting parallel between our religious

The Responsive Universe

thinking and religion itself. We seek to understand who we are as individuals, and all world religions seek to explain how the earth was created and how man came to be. Religion, aside from adding purpose and meaning to our often-indefinable world, typically also gives us a story about creation—creation of the Universe and also our place in it. Ancient religions were indeed born and based on subsistence strategies. As societies evolved, religious thought became more about mental conditioning and living morally, more of a subsistence strategy for society itself and for who was top in the hierarchy of power.

Now in times when technology and scientific theory is able to answer the "how" of how the Universe was formed, we still seek, as beings who need faith and spirituality, the "why" and "what" of why we are here and what it all means. As we move on to discuss the birth of the Universe scientifically, keep in mind that even in-depth scientific explanations of creation still leave room for crucial philosophical thought. The Big Bang Theory explains in great detail the beginning of time and the expanding Universe, and it also poses perhaps one of the greatest paradoxes in philosophical thinking. Before the theorized Big Bang that occurred approximately thirteen to fourteen billion years ago, there was no space or time, only a mathematical point possibly the size of a microscopic atom that comprised everything in the Cosmos. It is as if nothing existed before time and energy. And from nothing, came everything. You can equate this paradox with others that rule our lives—day and night, love and hate, heaven and hell. Philosophy and even science beg the question, can everything spring from nothing? We can define the "everything," the Universe as we know it, with beliefs and proven theories, but what is this "nothing" that existed before it.

The Big Bang Theory

Scientists and scholars can only assume what the Universe was before it grew to be a tiny dot the size of an atom. What is clear, however, is that in order for the Universe to have expanded as it did and have the radiation present that it does, we had to start with a very small, hot ball of energy. The beginning of the Universe is the beginning of time as we know it. Presently, there is still no widely-accepted framework for how to combine quantum mechanics with gravity (a notion Albert Einstein wrestled with all his life). Therefore, science is not currently able to make predictions about events occurring over intervals shorter than the Planck time. Named after Max Planck, the Planck time module is the earliest period of time in the history of the Universe, 10^{-43}, during which the quantum effects of gravity were significant. This 10^{-43} seconds could alternatively be written as follows: 0.0000000000000000000000000000000000000000001 seconds.

At this point approximately 14 billion years ago, the Universe was filled with high-energy density and enormous temperatures and pressures. It began to expand and cool very rapidly. Temperatures were so high that particle-antiparticle pairs of all kinds were colliding in a cycle of continual creation and destruction. At some point, an unknown reaction lead to a slight excess of the elementary particles quarks and leptons over antiquarks and antileptons, which caused a predominance of matter over antimatter, a tiny asymmetry that resulted in the substantial amounts of residual matter that make up the Universe today.

Science still cannot prove what led to the imbalance in favor of matter over antimatter. The preferred interpretation is that originally the Universe was perfectly symmetric, but a set of phenomena called baryogenesis contributed to the asymmetry of matter over antimatter which, in turn, created the Universe. This scientific theory rests on the age-old philosophical query of everything springing forth from nothing. The Universe encompasses everything—time, space, and matter. Nothing existed before it, and nothing exists outside of it, leading to a quantum number in particle physics of zero. But something caused an upset in this balance, an asymmetry that birthed a perfectly imperfect world.

The most current estimates guess that there are 100 to 200 billion galaxies in the Universe, each of which has hundreds of billions of stars

What we do know about the Universe is that since its birth, it continues to expand. We cannot visualize the Universe in the standard three dimensions with which we are familiar. The Universe is everything. Therefore, it contains the three dimensions of length, width, and depth, and also time and the possibility of other dimensions with which we are not yet familiar. Nothing exists outside the Universe and nothing existed before it. The Universe's expansion is intrinsic. An intrinsic property is a property an object or thing has independently of other things. It belongs to the essential nature of a thing. The Universe's expansion, measured by the metric expansion of space, is the increase of distance between parts of itself with time. Imagine a deflated balloon with dots painted on the surface that represent the galaxies. As you inflate the balloon and continue to inflate it, the dots move further and further away from each other, just as the galaxies in the real Universe.

An important feature of the Big Bang and its continual intrinsic expansion with time is the presence of horizons. Since the Universe has a finite age and light travels at a finite speed, there may be events in the past whose light has not had time to reach us. This places a limit, a past horizon, on the most distant objects that can be observed. This also means as space expands and more distant objects recede even more quickly, light emitted by us today may never "catch up" to very distant objects, defining a future horizon. The presence of horizons suggests that with the Earth as our vantage point, some parts of the Universe in the past horizon are too far away for light emitted to reach us. In the future horizon, light from distant galaxies has had more time to travel, so some regions we cannot observe in the present, we may observe in the future. Although theories that support the Big Bang, such as Hubble's law and Redshift, indicate that galaxies sufficiently distant from us are expanding away much faster than previously thought, meaning there is a limit beyond which objects will never be visible to us at any time in the future.

These theories point to a fascinating quality of our Universe—there is the Universe, vast and ever-expanding with past and future horizons we cannot and may never see, and then there is the observable Universe consisting of galaxies and matter we can see from Earth. To date, science cannot explain the absolute earliest instance of expansion. The Big Bang Theory only describes the evolution of the Universe from that point on. But because the distance between galaxies continues to increase today, we can reasonably assume that everything must have been closer together in the past. Because of increasing distances, we can also make assumptions about the Universe's future. Observations about the Universe's gravitational forces show that there isn't sufficient visible matter in the Universe to account for the strength of the gravitational forces between and within galaxies. This led to the idea of dark matter, which scientists estimate consists of 90% of the matter in the Cosmos. Dark matter does not emit light or interact with visible matter in any normal way. In addition, the Universe's rapid expansion and measurements of its mass density point to the existence of a large energy component within the Universe that contains negative pressure called dark energy. While scientists know that negative pressure is a property of vacuum energy, the precise nature of dark energy is still largely unknown. The Universe's accelerated expansion leads scientists to assume that more and more of the currently visible Universe will pass beyond our event horizon. Because of dark energy, galaxies and other gravitationally bound systems will stay together, but as the Universe expands and cools, they will be subject to heat death, a diminished state of thermodynamic free energy where temperature differences can no longer be exploited to perform work or sustain motion or life. More conjecture begins after theories of the Universe's demise: Are there alternate Universes? A "multiverse" with multiple dimensions that endlessly cycles from one process to another? Maybe black holes are the links to other alternate dimensions? Carl Sagan once theorized that our pre-Big Bang mathematical dot of energy may have been a white hole, the opposite end of a black hole. So perhaps the end of

The Responsive Universe

the Universe as we know it is just the beginning of a bubble Universe expanding from its own Big Bang? The point is, we just don't know. Despite all the knowledge accumulated by astronomers and astrophysicists, we only comprehend maybe 10% of the workings of the Universe. Further studies may trump the ideas and theories of special relativity we hold as benchmarks to our current understanding of the Cosmos. Or perhaps we will combine our understandings of quantum physics and interstellar gravity to form an ultimate law that uncovers the mysteries of the Universe. For now, we have our unrelenting quest to understand our origins and the awe of comprehending how massive the Cosmos is.

The First Mandala poses that True Nature is a spacious vision of the Universe to which we can all connect. The Second Mandala poses that this concept of spaciousness exists in the ever-expanding Universe, and also within our minds. The Third Mandala sheds light on scientific proof of this spaciousness and also raises the challenging paradox that is a fundamental truth in our thinking of the Cosmos—from nothing comes everything. Nothing is a property where there is no mass, no energy, no space, no time, and no life. One would think that in order to have something as vast and tangible, even if it goes beyond the limits of our observations, as the Universe, it could not spring from nothing, but instead have simply changed form to become the Universe we study today. This thinking puts a spin on that age-old paradox—there is no such thing as nothing; there is just everything. Nothing, or our pre-Big Bang state of nonexistence, the number zero, an egoless state of being in balance with the Cosmos, is part of the Mandala or revolving circle that seems to govern life.

No matter how you look at it, some unknown phenomenon sparked the imbalance that allowed for the possibility of life on Earth. Imperfections in the Universe, the upset of matter over antimatter, provided just the right variables to create conscious life. The concept that imperfection and imbalance are essential to creation is poignant in our lives as conscious, creative beings. As imperfect beings, often striving for "the good life" and perfection, we have created so many amazing things. Yet here we are at the age of enlightenment, so flawed that we have war, famine, economic meltdown, and climate change. Still, there is an imperfect beauty to the whole equation—the birth of a baby, a perfectly sunny day, positive energy and love—these are all attributes born from the interstellar chaos that is the Universe. Within the Universe's imbalance, there are perfect synchronicities that show us the world can be surreal and idyllic.

Humans are the product of over 4 billion years of biological evolution. There is no reason to think that the evolutionary process has stopped

It seems that perhaps imperfection as the essential force to the birth of the Cosmos created a world where the way of paradox is the way of truth. Night and day, feast and famine, life and death—the list of paradoxes that govern life seems endless, and ever since we had language, we have spun narratives to explain them. We still seek answers for the greatest paradox, that from nothing came everything, and with detailed scientific explanation still leaving a hole in the narrative of what happened before that first 10^{-43} of a second, we continue to look at reasonable conjecture and religion to fill the gap. The Third Mandala, however, suggests to us that there is no gap. There may appear to be a beginning and an ending to every phenomenon in life because that is the way we explain them as stories.

A different explanation to consider is that the truth of paradox isn't finding the balance between opposites; it is finding the revolving circle that binds them. In other words, there isn't just simply life and death; there is life and death and a re-birth of life. Storms rotate, seasons revolve; even planets and galaxies bound by gravity rotate. This narrative still leaves a gap in understanding who or what force set this cycle of life in motion, but the important feature of the Universe it highlights is that we have been born into an amazing Cosmos, and we are all linked to this web of energy that is immense and ever-expanding. This web of energy is our True Nature. No matter how small or insignificant we may be compared to the vast and intricate workings of the Universe, we are still connected and part of the equation. On one side, we have the Universe. On the other, we have ourselves. Not a balanced equation by any means, but the Big Bang shows us that with imbalance, comes a great potential for power and creation. Your True Nature within is that doorway to power and creation.

Meditation Session

In our next meditative session, we will begin again with rhythmic breathing. Breathing will continue to be the mainstay of all your early sessions. Once you feel your breathing is free of effort, focus on your body as described in the first meditative session.

Mentally travel from your toes all the way to your head, internally checking in on your limbs, your heart, and your mind. Do you feel pain? Are your muscles tense or relaxed? Being mindful of your body allows you to connect to something more personal and intimate. It also keeps your mind in the present. As thoughts race in and out of your mind, greet them, label them, and move on.

This time, try a new mantra which will help refocus your attention on your breathing: "Breathe in positive energy, breathe out space." The quality of boundless space is the focus of this exercise.

At some point during your meditation, visualize the heavens above at night. Call on that information you learned in high school science, and visualize the planets in the solar system. First visualize our Sun, blazing hot and the center of our planetary family. The Sun is so huge you can fit 109 Earths across its fiery diameter. As we travel away from our host star, we see Mercury. Dwarfed by the Sun, its environment is airless and strewn with craters. Minutes later, we pass Venus. Venus is about the same size as Earth and light beige clouds obscure its surface. Quickly, we pass our own planet, blue and teeming with life. We have already traveled 93,000,000 miles. We next pass the red planet of Mars and then Jupiter. The largest planet in our solar system, Jupiter is eleven-times the size of Earth. Our journey then takes us to the ringed planet of Saturn and the greenish-blue world of Uranus. Looking back to the Sun is surreal now. We have traveled so deep into the solar system that the Sun is merely a bright dot, almost impossible to distinguish from the myriad of other stars that dot the background. Soon we pass the icy reaches of Neptune and the proto-planet affectionately called Pluto.

We have just visually traveled hundreds of millions of miles in our minds. We visualized our solar system which is vast in size, but is a like a microscopic atom compared to the larger Milky Way Galaxy we call home. Here is a new paradox: We just visualized a space inside our minds so vast with past and present horizons that go beyond the realms of observation. Still, within our own minds, we can picture its structure. Much like the Universe, our mind is unlimited in space and capacity. In the theory of everything, God is the Universe. Western religion proclaims that humankind was made in God's image. Yet, our minds are like images of the Universe; with their own past and future horizons spreading outward intrinsically into space and time beyond the realms of our perception. To have the ability to conjure up the vast reaches of a solar system during meditation begs the question: Which is more spacious—the Universe or the mind?

Continue to visualize this amazing journey during your next meditative sessions. Marvel at the space in our solar system and within your own mind. This is the essence of space and openness. Your mind, like the Cosmos, is vast and infinite, capable of collecting millions of thoughts, actions, and memories. Stop and appreciate the boundless and shapeless characteristics the mind exhibits.

Daily Life Practice

Spend a little time outside on a clear night. Look up at the stars and settle into the vastness of the Universe and consider how it relates to your mind. We are products of the Universe. We can feel True Nature and how we are connected to this vast realm. Can you feel the spaciousness in that connection? Maybe you feel lighter and a little more liberated. Breathe in the night air deeply and exhale any fear of unknowing. Be aware of your thoughts right now. As you ponder this spaciousness, are your thoughts positive, negative, or neutral. Settle into the immensity of everything. If you begin to feel overwhelmed by the vastness of it all, turn toward the space within your mind. Feel the connection between that space and the space within the Universe. That connection is True Nature.

Look up into the night sky again. Do you need proof that God exists? Well, there is your proof right before your eyes! The Universe is God. We don't need to fully understand the past and future horizons of the Universe or dark energy or dark matter to know they exist. Conversely, we do not need to fully understand who or what God is to know God exists. So much of the Universe and God go beyond the limits of our observation and even our understanding. Where facts end in the narrative of our Universe, reason and faith begin. Gazing on the night stars is proof that something exists that is amazing and grand. God and the Universe are immense, intricate, and beautiful, and here is a new paradox: God and the Universe are indefinable but dependable. We know the sun will rise tomorrow. We know the stars will shine at night. We know we are born from the Universe (where matter won over anti-matter) and, because matter cannot be created or destroyed, we will return to the Universe. Life is not linear with a beginning, middle, and an end. It is a Mandala, a revolving circle, whose meaning is not the balance between its opposites, but rather, the unity of them. If this is not God, I don't know what is…

The Third Mandala

In the First Mandala, we discussed the importance of living with an open mind. The Third Mandala encourages us to analyze our belief systems in regard to God and creation. We cannot come to an understanding of ourselves without understanding our connection and place in the Cosmos. And we cannot fully analyze our belief systems without understanding their origins. Do your belief systems come from your parents or schooling? Do they fully represent what you believe about the Universe and your True Nature? Which pillars of religion best describe your own adherence to a belief system?

The Third Mandala shows us that the energy of the Universe, like our True Nature, is constant and unwavering. It is okay if we do not fully understand its workings. Settling into the vastness of it all and understanding that we are connected to it is enough for now. Once we settle into the vastness, we often find that the idea of organized religion for us becomes unnecessary and weighted. The concept of God and the exact workings of the Universe may simply not be understandable in human terms. The Universe is the totality of all that exists, of all that existed before, and all that will come to exist in the future. What an immense trinity! The New Testament in Western religion is based around a similar trinity—the Father, the Son, and the Holy Spirit. As you ponder the Third Mandala, consider a new interpretation of that trinity that transcends religion. The Father, Son, and Holy Spirit are different words for the Past, the Present, and the Future, or Death, Birth, and Regeneration. We sit in the Universe in the present with past and future horizons expanding rapidly beyond us. How do we explain it all? How do we find meaning in a realm that is so immense we can't even fully comprehend it? We find meaning in the connections that bind the paradoxes of life; the unity of the Mandala. God, the Universe, and True Nature are not three separate phenomena we must strive to understand; they are one and the same and you as an instinctual, conscious entity are a part of this magnificent system.

Third Mandala Exit Strategy

- Establish your very own belief systems about the origins of the Universe and evolution.
- Settle into the concept that the Universe is comprised of this immense vastness of interstellar space and sense how the mind may be related.
- Meditate on the immensity of the Universe and how it relates to your mind and True Nature.
- Mantra: "Breathe in positive energy, breathe out space".
- Daily Life Practice: Turn toward the vastness of the mind and how it might relate to the Universe – Look up into the night sky: Do you need proof that God exists? God is the Universe! It is okay if we do not fully comprehend God, just revel in its immensity.

The Fourth Mandala

The De-Construction of Organized Religion

The De-Construction of Organized Religion

The Pillars of Religion in the Third Mandala posed several reasons for contemporary society's need for religion: To explain cause-and-effect situations, social interaction, to provide a crutch in life, fear, and our genuine need for spirituality. No matter what the need is, all personal reasons for clinging to religious belief are valid so long as they are derived from an individual's own thought processes and are not the borrowed thoughts of another. Where the Third Mandala encouraged us to analyze our belief systems in regard to God and creation, the Fourth Mandala will take this a step further and challenge us to consider the difference between spirituality and religion. You may recognize a pattern developing as our Mandalas build upon each other—all are based around the notion that we all have an indestructible and unwavering quality within us called True Nature. True Nature, our minds, and the Universe are all boundless frontiers. Where knowledge and scientific explanation fail to answer the mysteries of our minds and the Cosmos, religion often picks up the slack, offering stories as answers and promises of heaven after death as long as we follow the rules of a determined "good" life. The challenge of the Fourth Mandala is to reconsider this boundless quality of our Universe and our minds, and to question whether this fits inside a man-made, structured belief.

Religion is expressly a vehicle for faith. Without faith in a religious order, doctrines of organized religions such as Christianity and Islam would be simply legends and parables. A faith-fueled merger of church and state is what has turned modern religion into the persuasive, money-earning juggernaut it is today; especially Western faith. Religion is no longer left to church on Sundays or Islamic calls to prayer. With cable, internet, and satellite television, apps and smart phones, religious programming is everywhere every day. It is now not just a vehicle for Kings and Popes, it is a full-blown industry that touches every aspect of culture down to our historical teachings. In the past, religion was an effective tool for crowd control as well as mind control. History and religion were merged as one, and religious authorities passed down "knowledge" that kept the dominant church in power. Without information readily at hand to question authority, the poor and less-educated masses blindly adopted what was presented to them as religious and historical truths without analyzing the source of the teachings. Questioning the validity of such lessons, after all, was heresy.

What amazes me is that with the infusion of television and internet into our lives, where research tools are now literally in the palms of our hands, many people still adopt religious beliefs that have not changed in hundreds if not thousands of years. The Constitution of the United States has been amended several times to better fit modern society's changing needs, but few organized religions have made any attempt to adapt from their archaic ways. Yet, many of us still accept what a powerful few say is the truth. We accept lessons passed down by our parents and teachers as the truth. We incorporate them into our lives without considering that these truths have been handed down to us by a small religious and political minority determined to manipulate the majority. Questioning these truths is the premise of the Fourth Mandala.

The boundaries between religious history and our chronological history often bleed together to the point that they are considered one and the same. I will use my own childhood upbringing as a simple example: I grew up in the United States. My parents were not staunch religious people. My family rarely went to church, and I attended standard public schools. Yet, American culture is so inundated with Christian beliefs about Jesus as our savior and the Bible as truth. I learned about Christianity on television, on the radio, and through friends and family. I saw politicians earn favor from voters by pushing their religious virtues more than their social and even political beliefs. Despite not having a strict religious upbringing, I still adopted Christianity as the only religion. As a child, I had very little knowledge about alternative faiths like Buddhism, Hinduism, or Islam. I had heard of them, but none of my role models, my teachers, or family spoke of them in any great detail, nor did I hear about them in any news or entertainment outlets. So I did not consider them alternatives to ever-prevalent Christian beliefs. The opinions of those who had the greatest influence over me molded my belief systems like clay. Even biblical stories like Genesis were considered by many around me as historical truths.

As I matured from an adolescent to a teenager, I felt deep down that there was something fundamentally astray with the religious thinking I had so easily adopted as a child. A deep desire to question authority arose. I needed to understand the source of my thinking, and a full understanding of the source began with knowledge of how this book of alleged historical truths, the Bible, came into being. It bothered me that so many people were being lead by blind faith. That the populace was being directed by such short sighted concepts and ideals: Concepts and teachings that were old and archaic and only created more of a division in humanity, perpetuating ignorance and mediocrity instead of self-evolution. As an adult, small nudges and hints from my inner voice took me on a veering path away from bibles and pulpits closer to my evolutionary goal. Then came my spiritual awakening and a new understanding of spirituality was resurrected from the ashes of religious dogma. My successes and happiness in life are greatly attributed to my ability to follow my heart wish and connect to something larger than manmade religion. For me and my road to self-discovery, it is more about deconstructing organized religion and all the cultural and social trappings it has created in my life. Religion is a major factor in emotional and social growth and as humans we need to revisit our beliefs on major philosophical and spiritual concepts and be sure they are of our creation. We need to confirm that such belief systems are working for us now and are not just dogmatic baggage weighing down our potential to self-evolve. I am not proposing the complete rejection of religion; I am suggesting we utilize the good parts—the pure teachings, and discard all the weighted doctrine and unnecessary propaganda.

My focus was primarily on the New Testament and Jesus. What I learned is that politics and religion often rewrite history. After the Council of Nicaea in 325 A.D., over three centuries after Jesus's death, the Roman Emperor Constantine upgraded Christ's status from miraculously mortal to divine. Thousands of documents already existed chronicling the life of Jesus as a man. Many consider these to be the beginnings of the gospels. History shows there was a clear drive to unite various Christian sects to help stabilize the Roman Empire because Constantine feared disputes in the church would cause disorder in the state. Constantine commissioned and financed a new Bible. This version omitted gospels that spoke of Jesus's human traits and embellished passages that made him seem divine. Earlier gospels were outlawed, gathered up, and burned. Other changes in the church and Bible included the formulation for the wording concerning the Trinity based on Anthanias, changing the day of worship from Saturday to Sunday, the introduction of Easter, and changing the date of Jesus's birthday to December 25.

What is important to note is that the Holy Roman Catholic Church was in business several hundred years before Jesus was even born. It was a church established by the Roman government, pagan in nature, in order to promote common worship beliefs and rituals amongst the Roman citizens in an effort to better control subjects of Rome. The disputes Constantine aimed to resolve with the First Council of Nicaea were largely over the relationship between Jesus and God, mainly whether Jesus was the literal son of God or a figurative son like the other "Sons of God" in the Bible. The Nicene Creed adopted after this council stated clearly that Jesus was the begotten son of God. It declares Jesus's divinity by stating that Jesus and God are of one substance and for our salvation Jesus was made man.

The Responsive Universe 61

The purpose of a creed is to act as a yardstick of "correct belief." The etymology of the word "creed" derives from the Latin "credo," which means "I believe." A creed is sometimes referred to as a symbol, or a token by which people of similar beliefs can recognize each other. What the Council of Nicaea shows us is that creeds of Christianity have been drawn up in times of conflict in order to define and redefine faith. The acceptance or rejection of a creed separates believers from non-believers, or in the case of the Holy Roman Catholic church, the faithful and the heretics. Formulation of a creed is an effective way to establish common beliefs and behaviors deemed "good" and "bad" by the church or governing power, or often times both. Adopting a common creed unifies people and gives them an identifying mark as a society defined by a shared belief system.

And what about miracles as noted in scriptures like the New Testament? Is there validity in regard to the miracles of Jesus?

Do the miracles of Jesus hold any water (or wine)? Is there any proof possible here? Perhaps not. After all, considered skeptically, for all we know, Constantine might have invented all of those stories. In any case, here we have the birth of consciousness, considered a natural occurrence. Yet right there under our nose is one of the most amazing miracles in the Cosmos. I invite people to look at the bigger picture.

Is there a need to prove miracles? Probably many people already believe in miracles: Earth's existence born from hydrogen, carbon and amino acids is in itself a miracle. Many consider childbirth and the evolution of man a miracle. The birth of a child, for example, is there for us to behold as something quite tangible. The miracles of Jesus cannot be proven; if you really want a tangible miracle, the birth of a child is itself quite amazing (or the fact that human consciousness even exists). Do you not agree with this?

The Responsive Universe is about facts and science and less about lore and fables. The main premise of this book is to bridge science with spirituality; facts and theories that build confidence and not blind faith. There is historical data and beliefs expressed in the stories and lives of Jesus, Mohammed, and the Buddha among religious and cultural icons. The point here is not to discount man-made religion entirely, but to have people come to the topic with a non-dogmatic eye, allowing themselves simply to question it an open-minded way.

It is important for cultures to believe as they wish, free from persecution, profit and social manipulation—it's their prerogative. It is called freedom of mind. This freedom of mind is the sovereignty to question authority and be free to speak our minds without discrimination. Only until recently has this social environment been available to Western culture. In places like the Middle East, freedom from religious persecution is still a major problem, especially for women.

It may be time to stress here that people can reach god through meditation, mindfulness, nature, and science without fear of going to hell (for example). If we look at the history of various religions, we can see that at times religion has blocked our spiritual evolution and growth; we need to address this (especially in the West) in order to move forward on our own path to enlightenment. This is an invitation to free our belief systems from blind faith and fear. There are, after all, many paths to the concept of God as it relates to the Universe. We can keep a belief matrix in place but is it the borrowed ideas of others? Is your belief system based on a book that was rewritten many times to benefit the few in power at different points in history? Is your belief system and system of right and wrong based on a fear of burning alive for eternity? These are questions we need to ask ourselves so that we can move forward and not backward in spiritual growth. Further, everything we need to know about God can be found within. My focus is for people to find god on their own through meditation and self-discovery. Nothing is more empowering; this perspective is for this reason (and others) very important to keep in mind as we progress here.

*Some research indicates that Jesus may have had a
spiritual awakening as did Mohammad
and Gautama Buddha*

I believe Jesus was a special person with unique visions. It is safe to say he had a religious awakening. Most major religions speak of such awakenings or "Kundalini" experiences where, depending on the level of enlightenment, an individual can theoretically become one with spirit and see visions of grandeur so different than regular, every day observations. Independent testimony of Near Death Experiences has also shed light on a similar phenomenon where people undergo an awakening and have aligned themselves with their soul and True Nature. For me, the Bible cannot confirm or deny the divinity of Jesus, but Jesus's lineage does not matter to me. We can extract divinity and truth from his teachings, not his bloodline. In spite of my skepticism about organized religion, I do believe in God, but I consider myself to be spiritual rather than religious. Religion is a set of beliefs concerning the cause, nature, and purpose of the Universe. It cannot be proven right or wrong; it simply stands by itself, feeding on the faith of its parishioners. Faith is confidence and trust in a set of ideologies. Faith can be learned, and that is the focus of organized religion—to teach what faith is true.

I do not believe organized religion is the only or most valuable way to further spiritual growth; but I do not think religion itself is bad. I think religion exists as a social phenomenon, providing a sense of community to people who seek answers about their life purpose and what happens after death. Yet, I do think that religion is a single window that sometimes obscures the bigger view. It provides a framework of logic, but misses the main premise that God is not a man, a father, a creator whose being and words can be captured and communicated through a single book. God is everything and is everywhere, and most importantly, God is inside every one of us; no matter what spirituality or religiosity we choose to believe. While I understand the benefits of the community aspect of religion, I think God is a private realm of thought for each individual and is an experience that need not be shared. I object to organized religion where God becomes a being who judges and doctrines become about exclusion. I particularly object to organized religion as a business. I think when money, power, and religion mix, we open the door to discrimination and a false sense of self and community. God is bigger than church on Sundays and a set of creeds and ideologies. God is the Universe. God is a vision that transcends all earthly possessions and limits.

The Cessation of Religion

A long time ago, ancient Egypt was a civilization ruled by pharaohs. Pharaohs were high priests and leaders who were considered half-man and half-god. Ancient Egypt dates back to 3150 BCE and through a series of stable kingdoms, separated by periods of relative instability known as "Intermediate Periods", Pharaohs ruled for more than 2,500 years. There has never been any other government that lasted so long. Egyptians and Pharaohs worshipped many deities, but none more famous than Re, the sun god. We know that languages die out. We also know that religions die out. How many people today believe in Zeus, Poseidon, or Re, the Sun God, in modern society? Even religions like Islam, Hinduism, and Christianity will eventually die out as new cultures and beliefs emerge replacing older ones. Over the course of thousands of years, change is inherent. If history can teach us anything, it is that cultural heritage is fleeting and transitory. Thousands of religions have served people for thousands of years. These same religions have also died with these people only to live on forever in textbooks and parables. In regard to modern, contemporary religion; a powerful question may be whether or not the invention of mass media and the internet will stave off such predicted extinctions?

Still, there is a quality to our human existence that transcends all man-made religion. It is our ability to connect to the vastness that is the Universe. That quality is our True Nature: Oneness that defines our connection with humanity and the Cosmos, from which energy and all forms arise. The concept of True Nature is the heartbeat of existence and is something that can't be destroyed or become extinct. Our True Nature is the unadulterated and unfettered source of instinctual energy that defines everything that is God. No matter what culture or creed we adhere to, within each of us is this unmistakable life source that transcends all dogma and religious trappings.

As stated before, I believe we are in a new age of philosophical renaissance. I say this because the collective Earth is no longer reliant on ancient religions to dictate what history is, what is moral and what defines our souls and the afterlife. Science is bridging the gap between the laws of physics and spirituality. We have choices and the ability to educate ourselves. We have been given the gift of intuition and instinct—thus an inner voice that can guide us to the truths that govern our existence. Above the social static of religious ideology there is a silent majority of people questioning pious authority. As discussed in the First Mandala, I call it thinking with an open mind. There have been people like this for centuries—many persecuted for their beliefs and philosophies. One such outspoken person was the third President of the United States, Thomas Jefferson. The Jefferson Bible, or "The Life and Morals of Jesus of Nazareth" as it is formally titled, was Thomas Jefferson's effort to extract the doctrine of Jesus by removing sections of the New Testament containing supernatural aspects as well as perceived misinterpretations he believed had been added by the "Four Evangelists" (Gospels). Jefferson was attempting to reverse the propaganda of Constantine and others that have manipulated the true words of Jesus. Fortunately today, in a world entrenched in mass media where information is at our finger tips, we are able to go back into history and read and research all levels of teachings and ideals. We are able see all sides of the story—that is, the story of our history. We are able to research other religions, study the Bible, including more ancient versions and ultimately make our own decisions about God, creation, and basically life in general.

With all the hatred, pain, and war in the world, people often ask the question, "Why doesn't God do something?" The answer, however, is quite simple. Bad things happen and exist because of bad people. Likewise, good things happen because of good people. God is not a force that operates on a human level. God is the Universe, and as we saw in the Third Mandala, the Universe is a system whose levels of operation still defy complete understanding. The Universe does not have a human conscious; instead, it creates an environment that allows for our independent, conscious thought. The power and energy of God is not contained in one supreme being, but rather, it is an instinctual energy that is everything and everywhere. Its quality is defined as True Nature. All humans are connected to this dynamism. It is what allows for all possibilities with the realm of quantum physics, including our ability for conscious thought. Religions of the past and present are just antennae reaching up to understand and appreciate the Universe. The threads that make up this metaphorical tapestry that illustrates God and Universe are all different colors. Yet despite the differences in our explanations for creation and the world, we are all made of the same stuff—the Universe. Our differences within this tapestry of story and explanation, while colorful, are insignificant. We are all here on Earth with the same goal—to revel in the immensity of everything and carve within the Cosmos our own life of happiness and love, to weave our own tapestry, colorful and long.

"Who is more humble? The scientist who looks at the Universe with an open mind and accepts whatever the Universe has to teach us, or somebody who says everything in this book must be considered the literal truth and never mind the fallibility of all the human beings involved?"

Carl Sagan

Our ego is a powerful entity that tends to hold our minds hostage. Attached to the ego are trappings of guilt and fear. Religion is interwoven into our ego facilities. We may feel trepidation and shame turning our back on a prescribed faith even when fresher perspectives in life arise. This is a completely natural process of self-discovery. To surrender your faith and walk away from the structure and confines of religion is a difficult and lengthy process. People around you will question your motives and direction. Others may feel threatened by your newfound independence. You need to follow you heart and continually ask yourself important questions. Does my religion really work? Does my religion provide reasonable answers to pressing questions about life and death in modern times?

It is crucial to find spiritual connections to your environment and community that are steadfast and unchanging. Instead of connecting to man-made creeds adopted to proclaim divinity of those who held power, connect to the vastness of your own mind as it relates to the Universe and your True Nature. You are a product of the Universe. You are part of the ultimate design. Settle into that enormity. Accept it and clarity will arise

The Responsive Universe

from the confusion about God, creation, and death. Diminished will be guilt and passive fear; empowerment and understanding your new step forward.

The Devil and Hell

Throughout history, religion has preached the merits of good and condemned the temptations of evil. Good and evil are principles conceived by humankind, and they exist independently of religions and theology. The idea of evil is unique to humankind, our species being the only in the animal kingdom with conscious thought. Animals do not have evil intentions. They kill for survival and weed out the weak among them through natural selection. There are no moral issues in the animal kingdom. In fact, there is no evil in the expanse of interstellar space. In the Universe, there is only energy that relates to the Cosmos. There is nothing evil about planets and stars. It seems, rather, that only the mind capable of conscious thought must wrestle with the possibility of intended evil.

Humans are conditioned to learn the difference between good and bad according to how it relates to society's survival. Individuals must decide what paths they choose in life according to their own personal thoughts, decisions, and societal pressures. Every day, people face situations that, once acted on, will either create a positive or negative effect on their lives. It is no wonder then that religion was invented. Most children are taught at a young age to believe in heaven and hell. We are told that we will go to hell if we do not believe in God and if we act badly. If we embrace God and act well, we will go to heaven. These concepts work reasonable well when we are children because we are familiar with the notion that good behavior earns reward. When we become older, however, and witness famine, war, and oppression throughout the world, we begin to question everything we know. We realize the world doesn't always operate on a simple system of good behavior and reward. This is when the treads of religious belief begin to fray.

I believe there is no fiery damnation or a Satan. To believe in hell and Satan would contradict one's faith in God. To believe in God means you believe in one uncreated being—the Universe. If God is the only uncreated being, it cannot have an opposite like Satan. God is everything; therefore paradox does not apply to God. Philosophically speaking, God stands for all things good and pure. If you strip away the good and pure, you are not left with evil, you are left with nothing. Evil lives on a human level, not a divine one.

The devil is symbolic and mortal. The devil's true identity is our false perception of life and love. The devil is simply fear and anger, a creation of our maligned egos.

Afterlife

As seen with the belief of hell and Satan, humans relate to opposites in the world like life and death, true and false, day and night. It is no surprise then that we think of heaven in comparison with its invented counterpoint, hell. Yet, we should focus more on comparisons between heaven and afterlife, concepts that are synonymous in many ways in religious thinking.

I think the best way to understand the afterlife is to first study Near-Death Experiences (NDE). Many near-death experiences have been recorded and describe a dreamlike world that is painless and full of radiant warm light, a heavenly feeling unlike anything experienced on Earth. People from all religious faiths have shared remarkably similar near-death experiences. Kevin Williams, a NDE researcher, explains that in a NDE, we are what we think. Thoughts are the paying currency in the afterlife. He states,

> "The near-death experience reveals the true meaning of life and it is this: We are here to learn to love. This world we live in now is part of the divine 'University' of higher learning where learning to love is what life is all about. The near-death experience suggests that life and love itself is what many people identify as 'God.' Love is the power that holds all things in the Universe together. Love is where we came from and love is where we will return. Love is the law of the Universe."

Could it be that we are put on this Earth simply to love? To be faced with evil and negativity and make a choice between right and wrong, love and hate? Karma helps with these daily life choices as we tend to suffer when we create negativity and prosper when we do good for the common person. These tests in life teach us love and compassion. The afterlife is an area of human consciousness we enter upon leaving the physical world after death; a realm where tests are over and we are left to feel the ultimate creative force of the Universe: Love.

*Ascension into heaven or a heaven
within our True Nature?*

Dr. Bruce Greyson, a psychiatrist at the University of Virginia, has studied near-death experiences for years. He has concluded that these near-death experiences suggest that your mind can actually function without the physical body. Thus, research has shown that lucid experiences can occur even when the brain is clinically non-functioning. Biocentrism expert Robert Lanza has stated that since space and time only exist as tools for us to understand the world around us—i.e. without consciousness, space and time don't actually exist—we don't really ever die. He concludes that death is a reboot that leads to all potentialities. Dr. Eben Alexander, a neurosurgeon and an associate professor at Harvard Medical School, has experienced an NDE. He was in a deep coma and experienced near brain death. His experience and research shows that there is more than just pleasure chemicals firing off one last time as someone dies. He muses, how can the soul die with the brain if, in the midst of being brain-dead, one had a rich spiritual experience? Gary Schwartz, Ph.D., published impressive data and preliminary research evidence for the continuance of consciousness after physical death. In his 2001 publication *Celebrating Susy Smith's Soul*, Dr.

Schwartz headed a double-blind study using research mediums who were blind to the name and history of the deceased (Smith). The results were chilling and helped shed light on continuance of information after clinical death—even days later.

Both the afterlife and dream-world are realms of the mind where all things are possible. In our dreams we can do anything, even fly and visit loved ones who have died. The dream-world and life after death means freeing yourself from all physical limitations and fully inhabiting the mind: A limitless realm of infinite possibilities where space and time simply don't exist.

Meditation and out-of-body experiences tap us into this afterlife, this domain of dreams that exists already within our minds. Such experiences connect us to our True Nature, which is a pathway to the divine. Author Bruce Moen describes the afterlife in an interesting way,

> "Perhaps a better way to say this is that we can learn to focus our attention beyond the physical world. Physically alive humans don't really leave the physical world to explore; they just learn to focus their attention beyond it. There are specific areas of the nonphysical world that are inhabited by human beings who are no longer physically alive. These are known as the afterlife."

The afterlife, or Heaven, is an inner place of tranquility. Jesus himself spoke of heaven not as a place in the sky, but rather as a place within us all. Jesus's resurrection was described as a literal ascension to Heaven, but if Heaven is a place within us all as he described, his resurrection is more of a metaphor for his completed inward journey. He did not go to outer space, but to inner space. He rose from his physical body to fully inhabit his mind. He shed his physical form and returned to where all things return, to the kingdom of heaven within, his source—love and True Nature.

String Theory

From a scientific standpoint, is the concept of an afterlife even possible? Yes. String Theory is an active research framework in particle physics that attempts to reconcile quantum mechanics and general relativity, or the theory of everything. String theory teaches that the electrons and quarks within an atom are not 0-dimensional objects, but rather 1-dimensional oscillating lines or strings. These invisible strings may be infinitely diverse

The Responsive Universe

with variables of inestimable time value. This suggests that other cosmic manipulations exist beyond the edge of our known Universe. Many theoretical physicists including Stephen Hawking believe that String Theory is a step towards the correct fundamental description of nature and the Cosmos. An intriguing feature of String Theory is that it predicts extra dimensions, possibly even alternate universes. There are numerous questions about the origin of the Big Bang inflation, as well as the statistical data that support the theory that the Universe is expanding even more rapidly than suspected—a contradiction to current mass and gravity data. Mathematical measurements of dark energy do not match current theoretical equations; yet, the concept of multiple universes supports the disparities seen within our quantum dominion.

String Theory is still in its infancy, and there are many more exciting discoveries to be made in the world of physics. If modern physics can prove alternate universes exist, it could very well be that these spatial dimensions are alternate realities or dimensions, including an afterlife. As we continue to uncover the intricacies of the Cosmos, it has become clear that anything is possible, because String Theory presents a universe of infinite possibility.

Black Holes

What is based on more substantial scientific evidence are recent discoveries in black holes and their theorized physics. A black hole is a region of space from which nothing, not even light, can escape. For decades it was thought that nothing could survive the plunge into a black hole. It is now a widely held theory that light and energy that is trapped in a black hole can survive. This is important because nothing is more violent and ever changing than the environment that exists at the event horizon of a black hole. Observable matter appears to be stripped down to elementary protons, electrons, and neutrons. Much as in death, we return to our source of elementary particles. Still, Newtonian physics states, in principle, that complete information about a physical system at one point in time should determine its state at any other time. In terms of Quantum mechanics, information that is created cannot be destroyed, even during the strenuous gravity and light vacuum characteristics present in a black hole. As stated earlier, energy and thoughts can be considered united and appear to be stable and transferable even when matter changes form. This means our thoughts can in theory live on after death.

Reincarnation

Reincarnation is a well-held theory for many. It is believed reincarnation occurs when the soul or spirit comes back to life after death in the form of a newborn body. This doctrine is central to many eastern religions such as Hinduism and Buddhism. Academic psychiatrist Dr. Ian Stevenson led the study of reincarnation in the United States until his death in 2007. Stevenson saw reincarnation as "the survival of personality after death." He believed the existence of past lives explained the human condition—mainly that some human personalities display essential traits that persist for some time even after death, existing independently of a person's former brain and body. He claimed that these essential traits by some mechanism would come to reside in other human bodies at some time during gestation or birth. Dr. Brian Weiss, former chairman of the Department of Psychiatry at Mount Sinai Medical Center routinely uses past-life reflections in certain therapies. In his book, *Many Lives, Many Masters*, he proposes that certain phobias and fears, even anxiety, can be rooted to past lives.

Since the Big Bang, matter has existed within the Universe and modern physics states that matter cannot be destroyed but can change form in a revolving Mandala of energy. The Universe itself operates on this principle—stars themselves are born from the gases of deceased stars. The emergence of seasons is a regeneration of dormant plant life here on Earth. Planets rotate, galaxies rotate, and the essence of time revolves. It is entirely plausible that the life and death of humans would also be a revolving door of energy. Much like our research and understanding of the Universe and the human brain, there is a great deal of clinical documentation supporting the existence of reincarnation, but there is still room for much conjecture. There are unsolved mysteries that still require a leap of faith but when we look at the Mandala of life, we come to find that most things within our environment are relative—a birth, life, death, and rebirth would be relative to our existence.

Studies in NDE and reincarnation help add a humanistic quality to what happens after death. Do we retain our human form or do we return to instinctual energy upon demise? There is this element of fear associated with death that permeates the epoch of mankind. Further, there is this undeniable thirst to know what happens after cessation, a question that has been a major supporting factor in contemporary religion. Still, the concept of God as it relates to the Universe is mind-boggling. For many, it is enough to know that modern science proves we live on in some form. The dogma and humanistic trappings of reincarnation, heaven, and NDE are promising and heartwarming, but true solace here on Earth can be found by connecting to our True Nature that exists within all sentient beings. As stated, True nature is a quantum-governed energy-force that is constant and unwavering. Much like the concept of a soul, our True Nature is an instinctual energy field comprised of waves of subatomic light and matter. So it seems that the best approach to understanding life after death is taking heed to the wisdom of few and then following your True Nature. The answers lie within and once you come to understand that we are simply energy changing form, gone will be any fear of death. You will come to understand we are a part of something magnificent and in some form we will always remain connected and pure like the energy that surrounds us. It is ego and false perception that have bred religion, fear, and notions of hell and purgatory. Once you strip away the ego and all that is adulterated and polluted, all that is left is energy—pure and powerful. We come from energy and we will go back to energy.

Auras

An aura is a field of subtle, luminous radiation surrounding a person or object. In recent years, scientists have conducted much research on auras or bio-fields. Clearly there is a bond between auras and our connection with the energy of the Universe. We are all made from this energy, and at microscopic levels, energy permeates our being.

Dr. Glen Rein, Ph.D., director of the Quantum Biology Research Lab, suggests that externally applied quantum fields produce biological effects at the cellular level. The bio-energy field or aura is composed of embedded layers of electromagnetic and quantum fields. As we will discuss in the Eighth Mandala, energy in the form of waves and light particles cannot be destroyed, it can only change form. Quantum mechanics describes a matrix of energy that surrounds and links all matter and gravity at the micron and sub-micron level. We are all connected to this energy field. So where does this energy go after death if it is not destroyed, but merely changes form? Answers to that question open the door to the existence of heaven, an afterlife, and even reincarnation, not explained by dogmatic blind faith but an emerging science that is just beginning to uncover the truths of the Cosmos.

*God as it relates to the Universe
and not just mankind*

The Soul

The soul is the principle of life, feeling, action, and thought. There is, however, a lacking quality to the concept of a soul. The idea of a soul is similar to True Nature; both are sources of energy, free from ego and suffering. It is an energy we can open up to and depend on. Like our True Nature, the soul is often regarded as a distinct entity separate from the body, one filled with God and all things positive. The soul and True Nature only parallel each other to a point. The idea of a soul falls short because of the religious trappings associated with it. In religion, souls are an energy source that can be taken away from you. For example, in Christianity, the devil can take your soul and trap you in Hell.

True Nature is an energy source associated with God and the Universe, but it is immovable and unaltered by evil. True Nature is indestructible and no one can take this energy from you. Even if there is a disconnection to your True Nature, it sits waiting for you; dependable and unwavering.

Religious thought maintains that we feed our souls with good deeds and positive actions, yet the slightest temptation can sully them or take them away. True Nature, however, exists separately from our thoughts and actions. It is the conscious, instinctual energy of the Universe that is always there, cannot be taken, and cannot be destroyed. Positive actions and thoughts bring us closer to True Nature, and negative actions and thoughts push us further from it, but our actions and thinking do not alter it or move it in any way. The edicts and rules that govern organized religion use the quality of a soul to manipulate people and their belief systems. There is nothing pure about that. Often times, motivation from organized religion to live a "good life" of prescribed beliefs and ideals is fear or guilt-based: If you don't believe, the devil will take your essence. You will be an empty shell of a person, filled only with regret, burning eternally in fiery damnation. The rules that govern the Universe and physics demonstrate that living a life more connected to True Nature simply just feels better. Connecting to True Nature is feeling love. The motivation there isn't living a good life because you fear the alternative; it is living well because tapping into True Nature opens you up to the infinite realm of possibility in the Universe. Not connecting to True Nature closes you off and limits your potential.

Death

True Nature exists outside our thoughts and actions. It even exists outside of death. True Nature is an unlimited source of instinctual energy. We now understand that matter is neither created nor destroyed, it simply changes form. This is true on a micron and sub-micron level; so it is safe to assume the same is true when we die. Our mortal bodies return to Earth, but our energy lives on in some indescribable and indestructible form. Death is a rite of passage in life. It is a response to birth and is part of the dynamics that make up this incredible Universe. The late Steve Jobs said this at a graduation commencement speech in 2005 (already knowing the full gravity of his cancer diagnosis):

> "No one wants to die. Even people who want to go to heaven don't want to die to get there. And yet death is the destination we

all share. No one has escaped it. And that is as it should be, because Death is very likely the single best invention of Life."

If you are forty-something like myself, you may often look back at your younger days and marvel at how different you were decades ago. In actuality, that teenage self you might snicker at is dead and has been for years. Through cell regeneration, billions of our cells die only to be replaced by new cells. So quite literally at the cellular level, we have died and regenerated multiple times already in our life. Still, within each cell is a metaphysical vibration or energy that constitutes our life force or aura. This aura or energy is indestructible. As our final cellular structure collapses at death, our conscious energy lives on.

"Seeing death as the end of life is like seeing the horizon as the end of the ocean."

David Searls

When we look at the beauty of life and love that in intrinsic to our True Nature and existence, you have to include the process of death as part of that system of events. Deepak Chopra once said, "The mind and the body are like parallel Universes. Anything that happens in the mental Universe must leave tracks in the physical one." He mused further,

> "There is a part of yourself that never dies; that there is a core quality related to human consciousness that is eternal, that is non-local. For that consciousness, it is impossible to die after the death of the physical body. Your core being has no existence in locality, in space or time. And because it's outside of space and time, it is eternal."

Fear of death is perpetuated by the ego and our false-self. The ego relies on the familiar. It is reluctant to experience the unknown. It will hold onto fictitious parables about hell and purgatory only to reinforce such fears. Death is a facet of the Universe and need not carry negative social trappings. We are a fundamental component in the framework and matrix of the Cosmos. Regeneration is part of that framework. In order for human consciousness to transcend our physical existence on Earth, our bodies must die. This human consciousness of which Chopra speaks is on the level of our mind and thoughts. Research from NDE, quantum physics, and String Theory, all point to possible dimensions within our minds that survive death. This plane of divine existence is True Nature, the tapestry that is energy coalescing and regenerating throughout the Cosmos.

True Nature and the afterlife live hand-in-hand. When we merge our personalities with the divine qualities attributed to True Nature, the result is authentic empowerment; a merger of what is mortal and heavenly in our lives. This is the goal of the evolutionary process of life and the entire reason for our being. We must align our personalities with True Nature to live fully in the now and the hereafter. We must connect to that element of a soul that is indestructible and is not muddled by false pretenses of religion, ego, and control patterns. Imagine the possibilities of mortal man and woman if we can settle into the understanding that we are simply a system of variables operating within one of an infinite number of universes, a realm where everything is possible because every variable is a meaningful part of the collective system.

Meditation Session

Focus on your breathing. Once your breathing is set, center your attention on how you feel in your body. Be mindful of the present and what is happening now inside your vessel of life. For a new mantra, try repeating, "breathe in positive energy, breathe out fear." Becoming aware of and eliminating the debilitating grip of fear in our lives is the focus of this next meditation.

As with the last meditation, recall the mind that is vast and boundless like the Universe, a space with no center. Think of this for a moment during meditation: All human formations are considered transitory. This means that with birth, there is always death and then rebirth—a revolving door of life and energy. It also means change is intrinsic to life; change is inherent to our human existence. In regard to ego and false-self, elements in adult life that we maintain as truths like certain religious dogma may not be the same truths you believed in as a child. And for those resistant to change, suffering tends to be the common denominator. Why? Because everything that is attached to you—feelings, perceptions, fantasy, and fear—these are not fully who you are. These things were not apparent at birth and will not be apparent at death. Therefore, wisdom notes that though such emotional trappings might govern daily life, they are not necessarily aligned to your True Nature. Imagine stripping away all these things you think define you—religious faith, self-esteem, happiness, fear, ego, guilt, even emotional love. All that is left is your universal existence—your True Nature: Your energy that cannot be destroyed, only transformed, reborn, and restored. Settle into that vision of authenticity. There is nothing more powerful! Once one is empowered by our true-self and feels the connection to energy and the vastness of the Universe, the element of fear will dissolve. Once you come to realize that you are a part of the grand design, fear becomes remedial and unnecessary. Imagine living a life without fear. That notion alone will give you your first unadulterated glimpse of enlightenment.

Daily Life Practice

The main purpose of the Third and Fourth Mandalas is for you to respectfully question authority and possibly even your own prescribed belief systems. Secondly is the need to find your place within this grand and amazing Responsive Universe and then live with a renewed confidence. We need to be wary of learned dogma and blind faith as it can facilitate confusion, guilt, fear, and ego; possibly obstructing true illumination. Deconstructing organized religion helps clear a path to enlightenment. Behind all the unnecessary doctrine and dogma is your True Nature, indestructible and unadulterated. Think of God not in relation to mankind, but in relation to the immensity of the Universe. When you shift your view to a more spacious vision, you will see that religion is really weighted and gratuitous. Maybe you feel your belief systems are intact and stronger than ever. That is fantastic. If your entire belief system has been turned upside-down and your mind is awash with unanswered questions, simply make space for the questions in your mind. It is okay not to have all the answers. Everything you seek is out there. The art of life is to open oneself to the energy of the Universe and relish the immensity of it all. Surrender your ego and false-self to the True Nature within. When you forge that bond you will find its wisdom and love satiates all no matter what. Be mindful of this.

I think it is important for humans to have some sort of faith. Having faith in something offers hope in times of despair. There is perhaps no problem in itself in believing in God via an organized religion so long as those truths are based on your own belief system and not the learned or pre-programmed beliefs of others. This said, I can add that I am a firm believer that religion and its trappings are unnecessary for enlightenment and our journey hereafter.

For the next few days, think about what you truly believe in. How did you come to this belief? Try to gently touch on what is important to you spiritually. And finally, revert back to the vastness of the mind and how True Nature cannot be destroyed. Think about this energy that is immortal. Think about how a large part of its immortality is its essential nature – it exists to create and change. And finally, see with unadulterated clarity that you are a part of this grand design.

The Fourth Mandala

God is a boundless orb, a sphere whose presence is felt by the mind and the senses. God's infinite sphere has a center that is everywhere and a circumference that is boundless. God is an indescribable celestial consciousness that guides and directs all life in form and non-form. With this in mind, we know logically that books and rules cannot truly govern our faith. The Dalai Lama summed it up elegantly, "There are billions of people on this Earth, each with their own individual, spiritual needs. It seems we need billions of religions, too."

Where religion often tells you what not to do, spirituality opens you up to life's positive energy and sets you free. When we look for the god within us, we become empowered and free of fear. As sub atomic physics explains, our energy born from thoughts and actions is the source of creation in the present moment. When we consider the concept of God as it relates to the Universe, we need to consider ourselves as of part of that definition. We can also see that we are part of a "True Reality" that exists beyond earthly possessions and religious trappings. We do not need to understand how everything works—we just need faith that we are an important part of something magnificent. We do not need ancient parables like the Bible or money-making vehicles like church to find our way. We just need to open ourselves to love, life, and energy, and know that we are connected to something bigger than ourselves, something bigger than life. By living a connected and karmic existence, we can live with confidence. Our confidence comes not from ego, but from our source of instinctual energy that is not destroyed in death. Our energy simply changes form, thousands of times in our lifetime and thousands of times in thousands of lifetimes after ours.

Fourth Mandala Exit Strategy

- Respectfully question religious authority.
- Establish your own belief systems about God.
- Find a scientific connection with the afterlife and quantum energy.
- Meditative focus on breathing, thoughts and intimate belief systems in regard to the Universe and how it relates to God. Remember that all human formations are transient and try to attach your being to something more fixed and permanent like your True Nature.
- Mantra: "Breathe in positive energy, breathe out fear."
- Daily Life Practice: Reassess and redevelop your belief systems about God and Creation. Journal your thoughts and questions and return to such quandaries later when inspiration strikes.

The Fifth Mandala

Understanding the Past

Understanding the Past

The Fifth Mandala involves looking back into your past and analyzing how life has shaped who you are today. This is an important facet in self-evolution. Earlier we discussed living with an open mind and how it is necessary to strip away our egos and control patterns to find the vast space that is our True Nature. It is these false projections of conditioned behavior that cloud our "True Reality." A clouded perception of reality causes unneeded suffering. The Third and Fourth Mandalas approached parables and religion that may have colored our perspectives on philosophy, evolution, and enlightenment. Hopefully you are working on building your own set of belief systems based on your spiritual needs and not the needs of others. As stated, much of what we have learned and absorbed began at an early age. There in the past, lies the source of much of the suffering we feel today: Self-esteem built on false-self and primitive emotions like fear and guilt are huge contributors. Now that we are aware of our True Nature and the space required to meet life's many challenges, now that we have gained awareness and freedom to question authority, let us take a closer look at the genesis of a dysfunction that lies in the past—it begins in our childhood.

All experiences, whether good or bad, shape us into the person we were in the past, who we are in the present, and who we will be in the future. It reminds me of the card game draw poker. Surprisingly, there is a metaphor here. Poker is a challenging game because it requires luck, skill, and psychology. It reminds me of life in many ways. Even if we have all the skills to navigate the ever-changing world, there are still elements of luck and probability involved. There are some things we just can't control. Our childhoods dealt us a hand of poker cards—we were born with a genetic code, as a certain gender to a particular family in a specific home town. Sometimes, childhood deals us cards that don't help our proverbial chip stack. Keeping with the draw-poker metaphor, however, we always have the opportunity to discard the bad cards and draw new ones. Especially in regard to an abusive past, we can discard what our childhood has dealt to us and sharpen our skills with the faith that better luck will come.

Positive and negative stimuli directly affect neuron development in the brain. This process begins at an early age and continues until death. Basic physics describes that for every action in life, there is a reaction. Energy cannot be created or destroyed—it only changes form. Any action in life creates an energy pattern that vibrates outward from the source and touches other people. Likewise, our actions are met with reactions that are either positive or negative. Your parents and mentors in life act, sending energy in the form of actions and experiences to you. Your responses are either positive or negative, depending on how you receive this energy into your conscious and subconscious mind. The energy from our parents and mentors influences how we react to situations in life here in the present and the future. They influence our self-esteem and ego. They can dictate how we conduct ourselves in personal relationships, our career choices, and how we raise our own children. An abusive or under-nurtured childhood will create control patterns that will many times unknowingly rear their ugly heads later in life. We must prevent negative patterns from becoming the circular models of behavior that connect us to people. In order to prevent future generations from inheriting the bad traits that caused us suffering, we must fully understand our negative control patterns and find the space to start making positive reactions towards life instead of default negative ones.

Author Dan Hurley offers a playful but resourceful analogy: "Two alcoholic mice—a mother and her son—sit on two bar stools, lapping gin from two thimbles." The mother mouse asks how her son followed the same addictive pattern of alcohol abuse… Perhaps Darwin would say it is "bad inheritance." And perhaps Freud might suggest that it is "bad mothering." Which is it? ….Nature or Nurture; an age-old question, right? Neurobiologists Michael Meany and Molecular Biologist and Geneticist Moshe Szyf offer up an interesting theory: The human genome has long been known as a blueprint of life. Family members can pass on traits including blue eyes, curly hair, or undesirable genes predisposed to things like breast cancer and heart disease.

Well, new research is showing that the genes we pass on might be more responsive that we previously thought. New insights in behavioral epigenetics show that addiction or traumatic experiences in our past, or in our recent ancestors' past, leave molecular scars adhering to our DNA. Molecular structures called methyl groups attach to genes, altering their expression. So, you might have not just inherited your Grandfather's large nose but also his predisposition toward depression or anxiety caused by the neglect he endured as a child.

This is not fringe science either…. Multiple independent research projects shows us that yes, we live in a Responsive Universe … and yes, our positive and negative actions and reactions can not only have an effect on us but future generations. This is where mindfulness takes center stage: As evolving, responsive creatures connected to everything, we need to be conscious of our actions, reactions, addictions, fear and anger as they not only dictate who we are but how future generations may live and be. The same can be said for those that are raised as positive, well-grounded children or adults, with wellness and betterment the common denominator.

Our main goal now is to look for any connections from childhood that could be affecting our decisions today. We all have experienced so much. Childhood memories could be fresh or they could be blurred or distant. You may even feel like you want to leave certain memories buried forever. Some memories may require the help of a therapist to properly analyze, understand, and deal with wisely. Our focus here is to see our childhood memories as colored sands in a bottle. We cannot sit and separate out each grain by color, nor can we analyze every single emotion we felt growing up. Still, we can look back and be aware of our more constant streams of emotions and determine the positive, the negative, and the neutral.

As children, we are virtually powerless as independent thinkers. We rely heavily on our parents and mentors for reason, spirituality, discipline, and answers. None of us grew up in perfect worlds. Those of us who are parents can admit that we are certainly not perfect, either. Let's face it: Life is not like a 1950s sitcom. Still, we need to be aware of how our childhood experiences shape us and affect who we are as adults and parents. The process, again, is not to isolate each grain of sand, or memory, and sort by color. It is to notice the color patterns, to recognize the good and bad streaming emotions that are rooted in childhood and may be linked to our actions and decisions today.

Looking back on our childhoods and finding understanding and closure from negative experiences is paramount to our self-evolution. This is what the Fifth Mandala entails. For those of us in our middle age, we may be looking back at decades that have passed by ever so quickly since we were children. We all have a path of suffering and resolution to trek on this adventure called life. Even as we look back at the past, we may feel stress even in the present with work and family and just keeping up with the latest news and trends. We also all have a sort of mental benchmark we've set to see if we're measuring up to where we expect to be in life. Are we where we thought we would be? Do we measure up to the successes of our parents or friends around us? We all have dreams and aspirations. Some of us are afraid to strike out and take risks. Some of us are cautious and calculated about our plans; others are careless or stubborn. No matter what you dig up in your excavation of the past, it is important to remember that our experiences are what form us as humans both from the inside out and the outside in. Our experiences are uniquely ours, and our reflections and interpretations of them dictate how successfully we are able to move forward and make changes.

Parables

Recall in the Fourth Mandala, where we found that much of scripture, particularly the New Testament, is a collection of parables. These parables get meaning or are labeled truths through interpretation and faith. A parable is a succinct story that illustrates a lesson in a simple way. It describes a setting, an action, and the results of a character often facing a moral dilemma. As we analyze our past and identify those situations that have most affected us positively or negatively, a helpful way to process our past is to think of the events that shaped us as narratives. In other words, perhaps the setting and the action of the situation that shaped you are like those poker cards dealt to you in childhood. Perhaps a game representing your childhood played out with a negative outcome? But now as you fashion this life event as a parable, you get to choose the result. You get to draw new cards and have the power and drive to choose how you interpret it and how it affects you.

What is our past, but a unique story that has unfolded in this narrative of life? There is a benefit to looking at our past as a story. As screenwriters of our own experiences we have the ability to rewrite history and in essence pen a happy ending to what may have been a tough or abusive childhood. There is authentic empowerment in knowing that we can change the ending to our own story. I strongly suggest journaling about your past—even creating your own parables or stories that paraphrases past experiences. One thoughtful exercise is to write down negative thoughts or aspects from your past. Put your past ills on paper so that they, even for a moment, are separate from you. See your past on paper, merely a parable of a time long ago that no longer influences or moves you. Then take those pieces of paper and burn or destroy them. In effect, put closure to such defilements and know that the past is just that—the past. Understand your past as a story in life and then begin to make small shifts in perception or in daily ritual that takes you in a veering path from your history—a more positive path.

*Abuse and addiction traits can be passed on
through DNA from generation to generation*

Journaling about the past and creating your own parables that describe past experience is therapeutic. Putting these experiences down on paper will at the least separate them from you. Try to see your past on paper, merely a story of a time long ago that could no longer move or influence you. Most important, be in charge of the result of the story. Focus on the positive outcomes. Only you can choose the ending!

Your childhood past does not need to be who you are now. True, you may have hidden fears and control patterns associated with these bad experiences, but you can rise from the dysfunction and rewrite your outcome to invent a better future. Realize that you hold the pen, not your past. You and your connection to True Nature write the final chapters in your life story.

Negativity

Many of our past negative experiences create a setting, an action, and a lead character in crisis. How we are able to analyze such experiences from our past determines the result of our stories. Again, the first thing to understand about childhood experiences that are negative is that they exist in the past. We all harbor our own demons, some worse than others. I have personally had several negative defining experiences in my childhood. These negative experiences I endured as a child continued to affect my self-esteem all the way into high school. The control patterns I developed would morph from one to another. Just when I thought I had my self-esteem under control, a new issue arose—an inflated ego. Unknowingly, I had replaced my fear and low sense of self-worth with a new false sense of security. I fed my ego, which in turn, satisfied my need for acceptance. As an adult, I noticed that anger and frustration began to surface, especially when I became a parent. This frustration and anger was directly related to how I was raised as a child. The first step to breaking the control pattern was my awareness that it was happening. Any time I felt frustrated or angry, I used this awareness as a trigger of mindfulness to stop and not react blindly. I directed my attention inward to my True Nature and made space for unbeneficial control patterns that facilitated anger and frustration. I broke the chain of dysfunction by connecting to this higher level of awareness. I realized that the negativity I experienced in the past was in the past. It did not have to color my experiences in the present. I had the simple choice of either back-sliding into ego and false-self—thus reinforcing my negative control patterns, or striking a bold mark by being aware of my energy, feeling, and thoughts and making new self-directed decisions that created positive results.

"Although the world is full of suffering, it is full also of overcoming it."

Helen Keller

Awareness

Awareness is clarity in any given situation or scenario. Awareness involves being cognitive of an issue and also having the openness and space to consider the best possible solutions. In the Second Mandala, we compared the vast space in our minds to the vastness of the Universe, both being realms with no discernible borders or periphery. It is from this boundless space that awareness arises. When we consider the concept of space in the

Fifth Mandala, we must include a new quality—the energy we put forth when we approach life with awareness. As we learn to reap the benefits of meditation and self-reflection, shedding our egos and false perceptions, awareness leads us to a voice of wisdom. This energy you hear speaking to you is your insightful True Nature; it is your voice, unadulterated and aware. It is a voice free of anger, ego, and hollow confidence. Awareness allows us to tap our responsive consciousness and not answer conflict and challenges blindly. It allows us to detect our hardwired control patterns that often govern us.

How can we facilitate more awareness in our lives?

- Live with an open mind
- Be conscious of your actions and reactions
- Have sympathy for your enemies
- Love yourself

Compassion for Your Enemies

I think we all understand that when we are in a good mood and things are going well in life, we have a general feeling of happiness that creates peace of mind. We can even discipline ourselves to focus on what makes us happy to perpetuate this productive peace of mind. Yet, harboring hatred for someone, no matter how evil he or she is, is unproductive. We all have experienced emotions of hatred; whether it is rooted in our childhood memories or someone in the present, this element of abhorrence is worth addressing. Just the mere thought of your hatred will overwhelm what was once an aware and settled mind. It will destroy your ability to judge right from wrong and throw you into a state of confusion. Hatred breeds negativity and control patterns. It is healthy to confront negative elements of the past and present, but it is unhealthy to hold onto hate.

Hatred is a mental cancer that will eat you up inside. Instead of holding onto hate, we have to make room in our minds to step back and evaluate the entire situation. This person you hate must have negative control patterns of his or her own. People who cause you harm cannot be happy themselves. We must understand that they are suffering in some way. Evaluating the situation as a whole and allowing yourself to feel some level of sympathy for your combatant will allow you to release your hatred.

Dealing with past hatred is particularly difficult. It is never easy for forget pain and sorrow. The only way to process this negativity and move past it is to confront it. In doing so, we become better able to understand the source of the issues that plague us. Many times, it is difficult to maneuver through the past because many of the issues that plague you are hardwired into your subconscious. The past can blur into a confusing and smothering tapestry of memories. If that is the case, therapy is a great direction to take. A therapist's job is to pick apart the threads of this tapestry through questions and reasoning. They have unique and effective methods to dig deep into the past and help us learn how to understand the control patterns that continue to hinder our lives. Seeking help is always a positive step in preserving a happy future. Creating awareness, understanding your past, and releasing hatred will allow you to make space to push out memories of anger, abuse, and pain, and replace them with thoughts and memories of positivity and happiness.

Meditation Session

Begin this session like all the others, focusing on your inner and outer surroundings and then your breathing. As your breathing becomes rhythmic and your mind settles, try to imagine a time when you were a child and someone really angered you—perhaps a parent, a sibling, or a friend. Isolate this specific memory from the past. As if you are directing a movie in your mind with you as the protagonist, replay the scene. Step back as a director and watch both sides. Evaluate your aggressor. Evaluate your reaction. Consider whether you, as a child, had any control over the situation. Often misfortunes such as child abuse are out of our control. Something out of control like the negative actions of a parent or mentor means we did not bring this negativity on ourselves. This means those actions were not our faults. Knowing that you are faultless in this negativity helps you understand that you were not that negativity's source; you were just a victim of circumstances.

As your breathing becomes deeper and more rhythmic, allow this memory of the past to fade. Release any strings of guilt you have attached to that memory. Find solace in realizing that you were not the source of that negativity. It was forced upon you, and now you can send it away. With each exhale, feel the memory fade even more. Feel its hold on you loosen. As it leaves, fill the space it left in your mind with awareness that you might have been powerless in that situation, but you aren't powerless now. Each inhale makes the space in your mind expand. Each exhale sweeps away the hatred and the negativity. Your mind is clean, bright, and aware. Use the mantra, "breathe in positive energy, breathe out ego and guilt."

Daily Life Practice

One of our focuses in the Fifth Mandala is to make space for awareness in order to break control patterns. Try to imagine a recent incident that angered you or caused your self-esteem to drop. Maybe a co-worker said something rude. Or your boss, spouse, or friend was unreasonable. Look back at how you handled the situation. Do you feel you handled it productively or that you said something you regret? Maybe you regret not saying something? Try to analyze whether your reaction was rooted in a negative control pattern or ego. Then use this awareness as a trigger for how you can handle similar situations in the future in a more positive fashion.

Remember, when we create actions or reactions, we create a system of energy that affects us and others. As you re-evaluate recent situations and face present ones, try to think of how you can send out positive energy from your decisions and deeds instead of negative ones. Try to avoid meeting incoming negative energy with an output of negative energy all your own. Our goal as we continue to reflect and act constructively is to gain awareness of how past positive and negative stimuli affect us. Once we gain this awareness and make space for positivity, we want to hold on to the good energy we receive and create. Focusing on positive memories and situations is the key to achieving a healthy lifestyle. Fighting and destroying, eliminating negative memories is not productive and is often impossible. These past events are permanently part of your subconscious, but we can continue to seek understanding of them and make space for productive thoughts and reactions to them. Most importantly, we can choose how they affect our game. We can address them as negative, deal with them, and move on. There are better cards in the deck, but we won't be able to play them if we hold onto all the bad cards we were dealt and time after time play the same hand.

The Fifth Mandala

The Fifth Mandala is about thinking and then making changes. Change is good, whether it involves moving to that city you've always dreamed of, finding a more fulfilling job, or starting a new healthy relationship. We cannot, however, make changes without first understanding the behavioral patterns instilled in us when we were children. We must gain awareness of what situations in life molded us into who we are today. Once we gain clarity from this awareness, we are able to change how these parables of our past affect our future. The parables of our past can either have meaning or no meaning depending on our new interpretations of them. When looking back at the past, try not to think of yourself as a victim of circumstances. Instead, look at yourself as a hero who has endured many hardships. Find sympathy for the people who have caused you pain. Try to imagine their suffering that caused them to act unkindly to you. Shift your perspective from that of a victim caught in a vicious circle of dysfunction to a hero who yanks yourself out of that suffocating whirlpool. Life can be simple like a parable—life gives us a setting and actions. Find strength in knowing that you choose the results.

My father brought up a good point recently—he said there is nothing wrong with working hard and feeling overwhelmed by the stresses of life. It's something we all go through. But he said the key to it all is to remember to fulfill your dreams. We can't let fear, stress, or any source of negativity hold us back. When we reach the golden age of life, we need to be able to look back on what we did and feel contentment. We should not look back and think a series of "what if's." We must always keep our dreams in mind and do our best to achieve our goals. Even if we fall short, at least we have the satisfaction that we tried our best. When we put out positive energy into something we are passionate about, even if we fall short of expectations or our goal changes, the end result will still be something authentic and worthwhile. Any effort in the right direction of goodwill and karma will result in a positive outcome.

As our childhood memories fade and our own children grow up, what will matter most is how hard you worked on your goals and how you carried yourself through life based on positivity and love. No matter if we were dealt the worst hand or the best, one of our greatest sources of satisfaction as we look back at our actions, is what kind of player we came to be. My father speaks from experience as he looks toward his seventh decade of life. He speaks about how as our agility and youthfulness disappear, we rely heavily on family and friends who surround us and we reflect back a lot on how we carried ourselves through life. He says we need to be able to look back on our lives and smile. I think his logic applies no matter where we are in life. If you look back on your past now and you can't smile, you need to make fundamental life changes right now.

A good way to start is to remember the principles of the Fifth Mandala.

- Live with an open mind,
- Be conscious of karma,
- Have sympathy for your enemies,
- Love yourself and others,

…and that smile will show itself. I make this promise to you and now you need to make this promise to yourself.

Fifth Mandala Exit Strategy

- Notice the mindful streams of likes and dislikes in regard to your past and recent past.
- Intimate focus on control patterns and effective ways to deconstruct them.
- Meditate on the past and work to release any strings of guilt you have attached to that particular memory.
- Mantra: "Breathe in positive energy, breathe out ego and guilt."
- Daily Life Practice: Think of a situation that could have been handled better—use it as a trigger for future situations. Then, think of how you can send out positive energy from your decisions and deeds instead of negative ones.
- Find compassion for your enemies.
- Understand the concept of awareness. Find awareness in daily life.

The Sixth Mandala

Understanding Loss

Rock Bottom

It was a dark, windless morning. As I tossed and turned in bed, the bright glow of the digital clock stared at me, telling me it was now 4:30 a.m. It had been a long, restless night. My wife and I were worried, but not panicked. There were times before when she didn't feel any movement. Yet, now nearing her seventh month of our first pregnancy, 24 hours had passed since she had felt our growing boy kick or wiggle. Sleeping is impossible when you're worrying about your child. The doctor said movement every hour was normal. That morning, Annamarie, my wife, didn't feel anything except a deep sense of dread: Something was wrong. There was some movement, but it was not the usual spirited kicks we were accustomed to. The clock blinked 5:30 a.m. We decided to call the doctor and head to the emergency room ten miles north in a neighboring town.

The first light of dawn began to show its dim face to the surrounding hillsides that dotted the community we called home. We drove up the highway as the early risers headed off to work another day. Strangely, this day seemed surreal. It might have been the lack of sleep, but I think it was a numb feeling in our hearts that told us today was going to change our lives forever. Annamarie and I had been married a year and were looking forward to the birth of our first child. I was amazed at how many dreams and aspirations could be tied into the tiny form growing in my wife's womb. As I exited the freeway, I prayed to God that everything was going to be all right.

It was almost 6:30 a.m., and Annamarie had still felt no movement. The white sterile walls of the Emergency Room were a stark contrast to the warming dawn sky outside. We waited as the nurse on duty processed our insurance card and prepared a room with an ultrasound machine. I looked into Annamarie's eyes as her own wandered across the bright room. Her eyes, once pretty and full of life, now looked tired and full of fear. They were bloodshot, and a small tear was forming in the corner, only to be quickly blinked away by her long lashes. I consoled her by telling her that I loved her and that everything was going to be all right. Just hoped I could answer my weighty promise. I prayed to God again to answer my desperate prayers.

She was a kind nurse, a woman in her fifties with blond-brown hair and a full figure. She quickly questioned Annamarie about how she felt and when the baby last kicked. After taking vital signs, the nurse switched on the ultrasound machine and began using the little sensor to probe my wife's belly. This is when time stopped and all that once mattered in life meant nothing at all. I prayed one last time as the nurse maneuvered the sonogram tool, looking for a sign of life. The screen that displayed the readout showed the silhouette of my little boy. Annamarie began to get nervous and asked the nurse if she had heard a heartbeat yet. The nurse remained quiet and continued her search. A cold sweat enveloped my body. I squeezed Annamarie's hand, and she glanced over to me with tears of sadness trailing down her flush cheeks. There was nothing I could say. Could this really be happening to us?

Days passed. I'm not sure what day it was; they all had blended into one another. I sat on a cold bench in the enclaves of mid-morning. The sun was out, but it was losing its battle against the morning's cold. I looked out over the bluff and let the ocean greet my tear-filled blue eyes. I had always found peace in the ocean—the smell of salt and seaweed in the air; the texture of the air as it breezed in from the horizon, the sound of waves caressing the seashore. Yet, this day, the ocean looked cold and harsh. The westerly winds whipped the salt water into frenzied white caps. The vivid blue water I had grown up knowing was steel blue and uninviting. Dark clouds ruled the sky and horizon with an iron grasp.

Like the wind causing chaos on the ocean before my eyes, my mind was in an uncontrollable tailspin. Just days ago, I had witnessed my wife give birth to my lifeless son. A small strand of amniotic flesh had wrapped around his umbilical cord and had suffocated him to death. The doctors told us the chances that amniotic band syndrome could affect a healthy unborn baby was one in a million. I was in shock.

All that I had dreamed of—holding my little boy in my arms, playing baseball, and watching him grow into a man and a father of his own had been dashed away. Like autumn leaves falling from a dormant tree, I watched the winds of change whip my happiness away, bringing a cold, heartless winter down on me. As I held his lifeless body in my arms, I felt sad for myself and felt a deeper sadness for my wife. Minutes after the stillbirth, the doctor allowed us time with our son. Annamarie watched me with puffy red eyes as I looked into my son's lifeless face. As she watched me say goodbye, I could not imagine what she was going through: To have carried this baby for six and half months and have to say goodbye on his birthday? It was all inconceivable. Would I wake up from this bad dream? We were good people. How could this happen to us?

Loss

How do you rationalize losing a child to a freak condition such as Amniotic Band Syndrome? Why were my prayers not answered? Why did God take my son away from me? I could not find any logical reason for why this happened. I would have been able to rationalize it more if my son had a disease or was afflicted with a birth defect that couldn't sustain life outside the womb. If that was the case, I could see how God would intervene, taking life because that life would have been one of suffering. Yet, this was not the case. The amniocentesis a week prior had proved my boy was healthy. He was perfect. Now he was gone. There was no explanation I could hold onto, no help, and no hope. This was not an unfortunate miscarriage either. We had to bury this child. Like replaying a horror movie over and over, I recalled holding my son's lifeless body in my arms. He was fully developed and beautifully silent. I recalled feeling the already frayed strands of my religion and sense of God unravel into complete confusion in the sad and tired months that followed. I walked through the valley of hate and anger as my wife and I grieved our loss.

"Find a place inside where there's joy, and the joy will burn out the pain."

Joseph Campbell

In the months that followed, I let go, but I let go to my hate and pain. I let go of any grip I had left on the love and pride that once filled me as I thought of my future as a father to my perfect son. I drowned my depression with alcohol, which numbed the pain but created a new dependency. Of course, life carried on as usual. I woke up. I went to work. I participated in the many facets of my daily existence to get by. I would go through ups and downs, but even the ups were centered in a shallow pit of melancholy. I was attached to grief, like a shackle around my ankle, keeping me from rising up and feeling whole again. Even at my worst moments, however, I did still have a sense that there was blue sky above me even though I could only see clouds and darkness. I still had within me a deep-felt longing to feel warmth and happiness again. I know now this was my True Nature, covered by grief, but still there, bubbling and percolating, trying to find its way to the surface again. I just needed to connect to its space and clarity.

Yet, even months after the stillbirth, I had no faith that things would get better. My horizons were still shadowed grey with no blue sky to be found. It was difficult to watch my wife struggle through her intimate and painful emotions. My sorrow was one thing, but I could not even fathom her loss as a mother who carried and nourished this child from within. Visualizing her pain was almost worse than my personal anguish. It was easy to blame ourselves—to think that if we had done something different, everything would have been all right. I recall it was my decision to approve the amniocentesis as eagerly suggested by our doctor, even at the quiet reservation of my wife who was considered a high-risk pregnancy. It was only later that I was to understand that Amniotic Band Syndrome is caused by the evasive amniocentesis procedure. For me, the weight of our loss now rested squarely on my shoulders.

My guilt, remorse, and negative energy was as raw as sunburn across an unclothed body. Blindly, we continued to seek answers as to why this happened. I knew my wife and I were good honest people. It could not have been a karmic issue. I knew our little boy was healthy; tests just weeks before provided proof. I had to start at the beginning and tear down everything I knew, everything I had learned from school and religion. Nothing provided useful information. No previous experience or applied knowledge could help me through my feelings.

I wanted to rely on God or some semblance of faith to help me, but my faith waned as each day passed. I began to realize that losing my child was only one facet to my suffering. The loss I felt became a conduit for other ills to surface—childhood memories and low self-esteem reared their ugly heads again as my life felt more and more complex. I started to lose faith that God even existed. God did not save my son from living with a debilitating ailment or condition. There was no mercy here. How could God exist and still allow such a thing to occur? How could he take a life for no reason?

Loss can be a debilitating experience – but there is hope, especially as time begins to smooth the ragged edges of suffering

Then, one memorable day in autumn, something happened that changed my life. The sun came out and showered me with warmth. The sky looked bluer, the clouds seemed whiter. The trees and plants all seemed brighter and more colorful. It was if I had poor vision all my life and suddenly began to see clearly for the first time. I experienced an awakening—I stumbled upon the concept of awareness and space and how it related to me. I no longer blamed myself for the loss of my son. I no longer blamed God or the Universe. I no longer blindly demanded answers for this tragedy. My son's death was an unfortunate circumstance of life. I stopped trying to find God outside me. The essence of God was not looking down upon me; it was inside me all along. God had nothing to do with my son's death—my son's death was an inexplicable process of energy passing through the Universe, a bright light that burned out too quickly, a shooting star. I realized I had never been close to God, but once I felt this loss, I came to know how precious life is. This realization brought a new sense of spirituality. God was the love I felt for my son. God was the pain I felt from his loss. And God was the renewed and fiercer appreciation I felt for my loved ones still with me. When I felt God as the love that burned with both hurt and joy in my heart, I knew I had tapped into my True Nature. Connecting to my True Nature gave me the space to experience my grief— I felt love lost and love regained and renewed.

Love pulled me from the perils of my depression and anger. After feeling such pain and sorrow, you wonder if you will ever love the same way again. You don't—you love more deeply. Ethan John Bader was born about a year and a half after the loss of John Jr., and his birth seemed like a miracle. Ethan's entry into the world did not replace my memories of my first son. There is no way to replace them. His birth, however, was proof to me that happiness and joy can still spring from sorrow. Ethan is not just my son—he is my hope and love for life in one form. I will always wonder what John Jr. would have looked like when he grew up. No matter how much time passes, there is still always a tear in my eye reserved for the day we lost him. Whenever I feel that tear well up, I visualize my son as an angel looking down on my family and reminding me to see the world with the same level of clarity I felt that day of my awakening. My son's stillborn death showed me how precious life is and taught me that love is the bridge between life and death, between sorrow and joy. He showed me a world of faith, beauty, and happiness. The sun will always shine brightly for me in his memory.

Letting Go of Loss

Mythologist Joseph Campbell once said, "We must be willing to let go of the life we have planned, so as to accept the life that is waiting for us." We all like to feel in control of our destinies, but suffering is a part of life. Trying to control our destinies can in itself cause or intensify suffering. Not all aspects of control are negative—a healthy level of control instills a productive sense of responsibility about one's future. Control does, however, cause problems when life rears unpredictable results like loss. The grief of losing something or someone dear to us is compounded by our feelings of helplessness. Love and friendship bond us in ways that create intense pain when that bond is taken away. Feeling love is part of our human nature: If we settle into the energy and bliss of love, we feel amazing emotions that envelope us. We often feel powerless to them, but this loss of control feels comforting and safe because to love freely means to trust deeply. We open our hearts to the ones we love, but we trust that our loved ones will cherish and protect us. If that love is taken away, our hearts are open with no shield. Gone is our trust, especially in God or the Universe. We feel alone and helpless. We feel angry. We feel out of control.

"Letting go doesn't mean that you don't care about someone anymore. It's just realizing that the only person you really have control over is yourself."

Deborah Reber

As we continue to make space in our minds for self-reflection and change, many of us need to create space for loss. As we make this space in our minds, we must let go of the attachments, like grief and anger over loss, that cause us suffering. We let go by filling the space we set aside for recovery from loss with memories of love. Letting go does not mean we do not care. It simply means we stop trying to control outcomes that are completely unavoidable. It means we stop trying to do the impossible by controlling all outcomes of life. The only thing we can control is ourselves—our reactions to unpredictable events, our attitudes, and how we move on. Letting go means letting go to love, love for ourselves and love for those here in the now and in the hereafter. When we let go bravely, we realize that while love makes us vulnerable to loss, it also is in itself our protective shield to our open hearts. It is our grip to our True Nature, even when we feel awash in a sea of pain.

Suffering a loss can harden one's disposition in life. Losing a loved one gives you a glimpse of how horrible life can be, especially those that lose a loved one with years of history to look back on. Everybody suffers loss at some point in life, some on unimaginable scales. The key to my recovery was realizing that to know loss and suffering is to know love and compassion. This is important no matter the magnitude of a loss. You can't feel a loss without having first felt something whole and wonderful. I don't harden my disposition in life; I harden my resolve to live a more positive and happy existence. No matter what suffering I have felt from losing love, I would never trade the suffering to have not felt the lost loves I mourn.

Trying situations test our resolve at the most intimate levels. Unfortunately, loss is an unavoidable part of life. Loss can weigh heavily on us, and at times, life may seem pointless and senseless. Regardless of the loss, people react differently and cope in their own ways. Although there is no prescription for recovery or quick fix, there are helpful ways to deal with the impact of a challenging life event. Below are some coping skills that can help in a time of need:

1. **Find Support:** At first, you may have an instinctive urge to retract from society at the hands of a loss. Many of us feel we need to shoulder our grief alone and not bother others with our sorrow. Instead, reach out to your family and friends. Ask for help with funeral arrangements or watching the kids. Use the people around you as a support network. You will find that most friends and family are eager to assist in any way possible.

2. **Seek Help:** Grief can be overwhelming, and there is no shame in seeking help from a professional. Signs that it is time for a professional may include prolonged sleeping or eating problems. Signs of depression, bad dreams, or anxiety can also be indicators. It may seem strange to confide in a stranger, but counselors and mental health professionals are trained in how to deal with grief and all its ramifications proactively and effectively. There is never a reason to suffer alone.

3. **Take Your Time:** After suffering a loss, many of us set unhealthy and unrealistic expectations for getting life back on track. You need to respect your need for healing time. Healing is a complex, step-by-step process. Take things day-to-day, and week-to-week. Time does heal emotional wounds, but it does take time to find positive closure.

4. **Take Care of Yourself:** Dealing with grief can take an emotional and physical toll on the body. Be mindful of your overall health. Watch what you eat and drink. If your body is healthy and feels good, eventually your mind will follow suit.

5. **Empower Yourself:** Use loss and grief as a source of empowerment. Celebrate your memory of your loved one by challenging yourself to be a better version of yourself. When you succeed as an individual, you commemorate your loss in a positive way. You are honoring the loss of life but fully living yours.

6. **Let Go of Attachment:** Grieving is a complex process that can lead to depression, addiction, and unhealthy attachments. Holding onto anger, guilt, or sadness is debilitating. Find a positive closure to loss. Be mindful not to destroy bonds of love by holding onto grief. Celebrate the life that left you by living. Use memories and thoughts of your loved one as inspiration to live more fully in the present, appreciating what you have because you know how it feels to lose someone or something meaningful to you.

Moving Forward

Like many people, I have lost both friends and family over the years; some very dear to my heart. Recovering from loss caused me to question everything I knew about life, and particularly caused me to question my faith in God and religion. Further, I could not reconcile how my perfect and healthy son could cross from life to death in an instant with no reasonable explanation around which I could wrap my troubled mind. With no reasonable explanation, I blamed myself. I blamed God. I questioned myself. I questioned God. But on that autumn day when the skies finally seemed to clear and the fog in my mind lifted, I realized that the chaos I felt in my heart was so complex and so visceral because matters of life and death are never simple. Recall in the Third Mandala that the mystery of the Big Bang is that some unknown phenomenon sparked the imbalance that allowed for the possibility of life on earth. For years, this mystery has spun scientific and philosophical debates on the ultimate paradox of life—from nothing came everything. The fallacy in my thinking was in attempting to find an explanation for why my son died before he even fully lived. The Third Mandala showed us that there is no real truth in paradox. Sure, our lives seem governed by them—life and death, night and day, and good and evil—but the real truth of paradoxes is not that they lie at polar opposites, but that they rotate in a seemingly endless cycle of rebirth, seasons, and cause and effect. The truth of life and death for me was that I hurt so badly because I lost a love, but love was the very thing that was going to heal me. Love could make me suffer and soar all in a cycle of loss and gain and immense sadness and joy.

The key to moving forward was realizing it is all a revolving cycle of energy. The Big Bang theory shows us that the Universe is immense and ever-expanding and that regardless of who or what set the cycle of life into motion, we are all linked to this web of energy in which matter is neither created nor destroyed. The Third Mandala put a spin on that age-old paradox that everything sprang from nothing. There is no nothing—there is only everything—and the closest we can come to nothing, to a pre-Big Bang state of non-existence, to the number zero, is to strip away ego and attachments and feel in balance with the cosmos and the revolving Mandalas, not the paradoxes, which govern life.

Meditation Session

We have discussed the concept of True Nature and how it relates to the vastness of the mind. Can you see how this relates to the vastness of the Universe? Energy cannot be created or destroyed and neither can we. Everything is connected. In this next meditation, try to tap into that space that is your True Nature. Understand how this source of energy is dependable and no one can take it away from you. True Nature can be your church, your temple, your sanctuary. Settling into its vast space means you have found openness for change and the facility to accept love into your life from all sources. If you still have difficulty opening yourself to this concept from the inside-out, then look for inspiration outside yourself. Observe good deeds of people around you. Remember the love ones you've lost and appreciate your love ones still living. Relish in the positive influences they have had on your life.

For this meditation, try a new mantra, "breathe in peace, and breathe out sorrow." Open yourself up to all thoughts of love—to memories of past loves, to the joys of love in the present, and the hopes of love in the future.

Daily Life Practice

I will never forget the impact of that one autumn day when I began to let go of my attachments to grief and began to heal. In Buddhism, there is an analogy that I think you can imagine resonates well with me, the "Blue Sky" analogy. Imagine your True Nature as the blue sky during the day. It's sunny, warm and inviting. This is your "True Reality," free of constraints, control patterns and stress. Imagine how light and free you would feel without the weights of evil, fear, and ego. You might feel weightless like a fallen leaf fluttering upward in an Indian summer wind.

Like the blue sky, our True Nature is constant and dependable. Still, life does throw challenges our way. Some things, like loss, even seem completely out of our control. Like the clear blue sky, our True Nature can be obscured by clouds, even by rain and thunder. The brightness and clarity in our lives can be obscured by things that are negative and obtrusive. Yet, we can settle in the steadfast vision that there is always clear blue sky behind the clouds. This means that all the pain, suffering, and troubles of life are fleeting. Knowing this, we do not have to react blindly in situations of conflict and suffering. Even the pain of loss is transient.

In the next few days, try to connect to this vision of "blue skies" and use it as a mental trigger of awareness when faced with a situation that causes stress or emotional pain. Try to incorporate the blue skies into your sense of space and awareness. Align yourself with your True Nature and begin to feel more and more liberated.

The Sixth Mandala

Whether you are dealing with a difficult past or the loss of a loved one or friend, if you do not handle your emotions constructively, you can be left with a debilitating handicap that will not only affect you, but those around you as well; including future generations. Love is what facilitates life. We are born into love, and we return to love when we die. We need to flood our lives with love in every moment; especially during times of challenge and conflict. Everyone's journey along the path to recovery is different. For me, writing and journaling are great tools for making sense of the conflicted feelings I have from past challenges. Seeing it all exposed on paper helps me communicate my pain and fears and understand what I am going through. It allows me to step away from the dramas and control patterns that surround me and allows space to fill into the situation. From that space will arise an awareness of how to cope; especially when connected to the authentic energy of True Nature.

Just remember, love is intrinsic to our being. It may take time, but have faith that love will fill your heart with reverence even after a terrible loss

Situations of past challenges and loss remind us that nothing is simple and that life seems governed by conflict and opposites. Remember the blue sky analogy that describes clouds as our challenges and conflicts; the blue sky being our steadfast True Nature: The blue skies analogy reminds us that while we may feel like situations in life are black or white, good or bad, or life and death, they are far more cyclical. Our earth rotates, the entire solar system rotates, seasons and storms all rotate. Even our concept of time follows a circle as hands of the clock advance to count each passing second, minute, and hour. Welcome to the Mandala of life—a sphere or circle of energy: Your journey of birth, life, death and rebirth. Sometimes an easy explanation or story cannot bind matters of life and death for us. We cannot assign logic and narratives to these unforeseen events that defy reasonable explanations.

In all this confusion, one thing is certain—circular patterns, not paradoxes, describe and govern our Universe. Love is one of life's ultimate circular bonds because we are born to love and we return to love when we die. Love can cause us life's greatest joy and also life's greatest sorrow. It is our blue skies and also our heart's most tumultuous storm. Most importantly, love is what will ultimately heal us as we process a painful past. We will find comfort in our memories of love and of the love we lost. We will find support in the love of those we reach out to. We will find inspiration in the love we have for those still with us. We will honor lost love by loving ourselves and our life enough to let go of attachments that cloud our vision with pain and suffering. Be mindful that any challenge in life, no matter how insurmountable, will eventually succumb to love in all facets. It is simply how the Universe operates. Have faith in that notion and make it a reality!

Sixth Mandala Exit Strategy

- Find love in life to heal the abyss loss leaves behind.
- Journal your thoughts and return to them later with a renewed perspective.
- Meditative focus on working to connect to that space that is your True Nature. Love comes in many forms. Try to connect to the love of people, places, and things.
- Mantra: "Breathe in peace, breathe out sorrow."
- Daily Life Practice: Live your daily life knowing that there is always blue sky behind clouds of negativity. The analogy of "blue skies" is much like our True Nature: Dependable and constant.

The Seventh Mandala

Living Healthy through Mind and Body

Connecting the Mind and Body as One

We now understand that positive thoughts and actions create and increase our connection to True Nature, thus improving our quality of life and wellness. When we are mindful of our actions, reactions and control patterns we create the space necessary for self-discovery. Through mindfulness, we are connecting the body and mind as one. Here in the Seventh Mandala, we will discuss simple ways to increase our wellness. When we are happy and healthy, we have confidence and high self-worth. We feel our life has purpose. We are able to handle pressure and conflict with greater authority. Stress and depression are simply unnecessary default instincts and coping mechanisms. So, why not explore as many ways to maintain a high level of positive energy and wellness in our minds and bodies?

Diet

Simply put, a healthy body requires good nutrition. You mother wasn't kidding when she told you to eat your fruits and vegetables. They are full of vitamins, minerals, antioxidants, helpful enzymes, and phytochemicals that strengthen our immune systems and even impede the development of degenerative diseases such as heart disease and cancer. Typically, our medical professionals today are trained to diagnose and treat problems as they arise. Think about it, when you go to the doctor, it is usually because you have an ailment. Most of us maybe make it to the doctor once a year for a routine physical or because we got sick or hurt. Our medical system is geared towards treatment instead of wellness. Eating well is one of the easiest ways to promote overall wellness within our bodies and avoid ailments like high blood pressure and inflammation that can lead to avoidable conditions. Monitoring what we eat not only increases physical health, it also makes us feel better, think clearer, and promotes a psychological wellness as well; we are in charge of how we feel when we take charge of what we eat. When we eat well and feel better, we are happier about ourselves and about life in general, thus increasing positive energy within and around us.

Here are ten easy steps to eating healthier:

1. **Eat more fruits and vegetables:** Conversely, eat less fried and processed foods. Fruits and vegetables protect against cancer, heart disease, and even have anti-aging effects. Though processed foods

are tempting because they are easy as well as tasty, they contain ingredients; typically the ones on the labels that we can't pronounce which literally clog our systems with toxins.

2. **Eat more "Super Foods"** like salmon, walnuts, and dark chocolate. Fruits and vegetables that are rich in color like blueberries, red peppers, and tomatoes also pack a nutritional punch. Vegetables of darker green hues such as kale and spinach are rich in antioxidants and help fight free radicals in the blood stream.

3. **Add a multi-vitamin to your daily diet:** We can't always eat well, and adding a multi-vitamin to your diet ensures you're getting the vitamins and minerals you need daily to be healthy. Even better, look for "whole food" supplements over laboratory derived vitamins.

4. **Meatless Mondays:** If you eat meat on a regular basis, try going without it for one day of the week. Meat or animal proteins should be eaten in moderation. Eating less meat is better for your body and for the environment.

5. **Super-size need not apply:** Limit your portions at all meals. Slow your intake and don't eat a large portion if you are not very hungry. Try eating three-fourths of your meal and then wait five minutes. You will find there is a delayed response from the stomach telling the brain it's full. Doing this will ensure you don't leave the dinner table with that uncomfortable, too-full feeling.

6. **Shop smart:** Visit the produce aisle. Skip the snacks and sugary juices and sodas. If you do not buy it, you will not eat and drink it!

7. **Curb the sugar:** Limit how much refined sugar you eat. It's high in calories and devoid of nutrients. Even better, stay away from products that use "high fructose corn sugar". Also, snack smart: Go for nuts and dried fruit over chips and candy bars.

8. **Go organic:** Choosing organic means you are eating foods that were cultivated without pesticides or hormones. It is more expensive to go organic, but pesticides and hormones have been linked with cancer and other diseases.

9. **Drink more water:** Our bodies are made up of mostly water, and drinking 8-10 glasses a day is important for hydration and for flushing out your organs and cells.

Eating fresh fruits and vegetables is just one important step to wellness

10. **Juice before dinner:** Make your own juice and drink a glass before dinner. Fill up with antioxidants and fiber so you aren't tempted to reach for the options that are loaded with empty calories.

Juicing Recipe:

1 banana without the peel
A small handful of fresh or frozen blueberries
1 cored apple
A small handful of fresh kale or spinach
1 carrot
1 celery stalk
A small sliver of beet
A dash of chia seeds
A couple ice cubes and a splash of water

Combine using a juicer or blender

Routine Exercise

Exercise relieves stress, helps regulate weight, and improves attitude and mental clarity. Regular exercise routines enhance healthy eating habits and encourage us to stay on healthier paths. Since we feel better and look better when we exercise, we also tend to want healthier food options. If you feel that you are in a lifestyle rut, devoid of wellness, there is hope for change. Gone are the days of eating fast-food and sometimes wishing for rain so you can slump on the couch and watch TV. Instead, with the right drive and focus, you may find yourself craving healthier food and anxiously awaiting a walk with your dog after work. If you're just starting to set a new routine, don't go out and run five miles and eat a bag of raw carrots. Instead, start small and smart. Slowly work yourself into a new lifestyle change. Remember, there is no rush in changing your lifestyle to a healthier path. Any new positive steps are better than nothing. A couple small healthy changes to your day will compound over time.

Here are some helpful tips for setting up a low-impact exercise regime:

1. **Baby steps:** Try a beginner yoga or pilates class, or even walk or take a jog. Work your way slowly into a more aggressive routine. Running 10 miles your first day of exercise ensures failure and also is not healthy. Repetition and building your routine over time is what will yield results.

2. **Commit for one month:** Make a commitment to work out three days a week for one month. This will solidify the exercise habit and give you an end-goal. Once you reach your one month benchmark, be mindful of how you feel and set a new goal that builds on what you have already achieved. Then, advance to a harder exercise class; increase your speed or length in your jog or run. Maybe even pick up the next heaviest weights in the set.

3. **Don't quit:** Most good things in life are not easy and we have to work for them. Push yourself to exercise. Push yourself to get to the gym. Push yourself to do five more minutes on the treadmill. Good things will come from this hard work.

4. **Use exercise as stress relief:** Instead of popping another anti-anxiety pill or having a glass of wine to cope with a hard day, use exercise as your new outlet. A little exhalation of stress and rage in a kickboxing class goes a long way.

5. **Habits first, not exercise equipment:** Purchasing expensive exercise equipment does not establish a habit for exercise. Build a routine first and then decide months later whether it's cost effective to purchase equipment.
6. **Get creative:** There are many ways to exercise besides going to the gym. Try riding a bike, going for a hike, or doing some gardening to break up a routine that is beginning to feel monotonous. If you can turn housecleaning into cardio, then both your home and heart will benefit greatly.
7. **Find an exercise buddy:** Grab a friend or neighbor to join you. Adding a social aspect to exercise can boost your commitment to the exercise habit.
8. **Isolate your weakness:** Is adhering to an exercise regiment a losing battle for you? Do you not enjoy exercising? Is there no time? Maybe it is feeling self-conscious at the gym? Be mindful of what is holding you back. As soon as you can isolate your weakness, you can make steps to improve the situation.
9. **Drink water:** It is important to stay hydrated during any exercise session.
10. **Make it fun:** There are countless ways to exercise and have fun doing it. Maybe it is swimming, walking at sunset, entering in a jog for charity. Even watching your favorite TV show while on the treadmill. Exercise does not have to be boring.

Music

Listening to music has healing effects. Rhythm, melody, and lyrics can help relax you, build concentration and memorization, and create positive energy. In the course of human cultural evolution, music has always been an ingredient to building closer interpersonal relationships between people.

"Music is the mediator between the spiritual and the sensual life."

Ludwig van Beethoven

Music is unique in its sensory appeal, and it also is an important and healthy vehicle for non-verbal expression. Music inspires an emotional response from its listeners that unifies people and also has personal therapeutic benefits. Rhythm and melody creates energy and draws emotions out, encouraging creativity and a release of stress. Music can also quiet the mind during meditative sessions.

Aromatherapy

We have talked about how effects like music and love can evoke an emotional and positive reaction in life. Our senses are corridors for sensory connections. As we will discuss later, healing touch or simply Bio-Energy therapies like Reiki can encourage wellness from a holistic sense. So what about our sense of smell? Aromatherapy can include incents, oils, and even candles. Aromatherapy has ancient origins dating back over 3000 years as noted in early Indian Vedic manuscripts. Aromatherapy oils are the healthiest means of enjoying the healing and relaxing qualities of the sense of smell. Aroma mediums like potpourri, essential oil burners or soy based candles, can deliver the perfect environment for a number of needs and ailments. Whether you combine aromatherapy with massage, meditation or to simply unwind, there are many exquisite blends available to stimulate or sedate your environment:

Meditative Herbs and Oils:

Chamomile: A mellow scent/taste to relieve tension, headaches, insomnia and digestive issues.

Geranium: Rose scented to help with depression and tension.

Jasmine: Mood lifter and invigorates spirit and energy.

Lavender: Soothing scent that is great for headaches and relaxation.

Lemon: Citrus used to boost immune system and great for skin as well as mental clarity.

Peppermint: Excellent for digestive issues.

Pine: Clears inhalation passages and is great for relieving fatigue.

Sage: Provides euphoric lift and known to clear negative energy out of closed spaces.

Sandalwood: Earthy tones to help relaxation, antidepressant and a potential aphrodisiac.

Ylang Ylang: Sweet smelling to help with anxiety, insomnia and is also known as an aphrodisiac.

There are many great herbs and essential oils available that are not listed above. The fun is in experimenting with which scents speak to you and facilitate energy in its many forms. Many of the available aromatherapy scents can be mixed and combined to create the perfect concoction for all your holistic needs. Explore aromatherapy and get creative!

Detox Bath

Looking for relaxation or meditative respite? Take aromatherapy to the next level with a soothing and healing detox bath: Dissolve an ample amount of sea salt in a comfortable bathtub with water as warm as you can handle (not for pregnant women, children, or people with heart ailments). Add a generous measure of essential oil (preferably lavender or chamomile to contribute to relaxation) into the bath allowing it to diffuse with the sea salt and bath water. While soaking in the warm bath drink cool water to keep hydrated and feel free to listen to meditative music conducive to relaxation. Settle in a meditative respite for approximately 15 minutes to a half-hour. Gently towel dry and remain inactive for at least a half hour after the bath.

Moderation

Moderation is the balance between something intense and something not intense at all. Often times in our lives moderation is a constant practice of self-management—endless vigilance and personal responsibility. Whether we monitor our alcohol, eating, exercise, or even our actions toward others and ourselves, moderation is a gauge of awareness that we cannot overlook. I believe almost anything in moderation is okay as long as it does not hurt you or harm others. For our efforts with the Nine Mandalas, moderation is a balance of energies. Just as we question our belief systems and behavioral patterns, we must question our needs and wants and see if they result from addiction, compulsive tendencies or deep-rooted control patterns. Further, we need to determine if such tendencies are rooted in ego and false-self and work toward that bridge of moderation. If you are indulging in a vice such as alcohol or drugs to remedy a trauma or deep-rooted control pattern, you are only reinforcing negative scripts and becoming reliant on something that only makes matters worse.

"The brief elation we experience appeasing sensual impulses is very close to what the drug addict feels when indulging his or her habit. Temporary relief is soon followed by a craving for more. And in just the same way that taking drugs in the end only causes trouble, so too does much of what we undertake to fulfill our immediate sensory desires. We must acknowledge that there can be no hope of gratifying the senses permanently. At best, the happiness we derive from eating a good meal can only last until the next time we are hungry."

Dalai Lama

It is up to each individual to regulate their own levels of moderation and determine what indulgences are positive or negative based on his or her personal situation. Use a simple trigger of mental awareness in situations that require moderation: Ask yourself, do I really need this? Do I need another drink right now even though I'm buzzed? Do I need to finish this burrito even though my stomach is full? Simple self-directed questions will help make better self-directed decisions so that we avoid actions that lead to suffering. The key is to set mental triggers and to also listen to them when they sound. Remember, mindfulness solicits moderation; excessiveness creates suffering.

Love Yourself First

Some of us find it hard to love ourselves. What does that really mean to love ourselves? It can be easy to find faults in who we think we are. Maybe you think you are unorganized or have a couple of bad habits. Maybe you get stressed out easily or are taking a medication for depression or anxiety. Maybe you wish you ate healthier or exercised more. Maybe you do not like crowds or being the center of attention. Maybe you love being the center of attention, basking in the glow of others' energy. We tend to look at ourselves in the mirror and not approve of what we see in the reflection, many times unknowingly. We have lived under the influence of such control patterns since early adolescence and passive self-loathing is a major facet of western culture. All of this self-loathing is rooted in our egos and false perceptions. It can make us want to be someone else or to berate ourselves as if we are unworthy and unlovable. It is one thing to love who you are and it is a completely different thing to love what you are. There is a fundamental difference to be actualized. Our perception of who we are is rooted in societal pressures: What we see on television, in print ads, etc. Our happiness is regulated by a shallow self-esteem and the approval of others. But what about loving what we are?

This is another kind of love. In fact, it is a completely different way to love yourself, and this other kind of love transcends all the controlled chaos that envelops our busy lives. We now understand that we are products of the Universe and thus are born from quantum positive energy. There is a quality to this that is pure and unfettered. We are the sons and daughters of vibration, light and love and that is something no one can take away from you. This is our True Nature, vast, boundless, and reliable. It is easy to love yourself when you look at where the source of our being is rooted (True Nature). Look up at night and marvel at the stars. Appreciate nature and the love for a pet or child. This is a love that is all-powerful and unchanging. Put your confidence into this type of love and soon you will realize all of your shortcomings in life, all of your bad habits and your self-loathing, are just products of a self-esteem driven by ego. Such worries and deceptions will seem trivial and unnecessary once you find empowerment from an inner source.

There is nothing confident and steadfast about our egos. Much like money, the ego comes and goes and for many it regulates our happiness and suffering. The more control we take away from the ego, the more we connect to the steadfast vision that is our True Nature. Love what you are (a product of the Universe born from love and energy) and happiness and confidence will root itself in your life. Once you have this unadulterated confidence of what you are, soon your perspectives in life will change. Soon you will make little changes in life such as eating better, exercising, or getting more organized. Soon, very soon, you will connect that love of what you are and who you are as one—a quality of oneness bathed under the light of self-actualization and enlightenment.

Happiness is more fun when you can share it with a loved one. If you have not met your soul mate, have patience and someone special will walk into your life when you least expect it

Love and Relationships

I wish I could say I had all the answers when it comes to relationships, but in the seemingly infinite world of love, marriage, and interpersonal emotions, the variables seem endless. When we see the divorce rate in America rising to almost 50%, it not only saddens me, but it puzzles me as well. We understand with some certainty that humans are mostly monogamous creatures and yet there is potential for much strife and adultery in relationships. Is this ego-driven or human nature? There are good arguments and research to support both ideas here. The answers may be varied from situation-to-situation and person-to-person. So why does any of this even matter? Multiple or failed relationships over the course of a short period would seem benign, but when we look at the karma, lost energy, and emotional toll; when we drag the children we have fostered into such hardship and through broken homes, we should ponder the long term effects of such adversity. One thing I do know is that in order for good things to happen to us in life, we must constantly strive to be better ourselves. We must also always be aware of our environment and how we present ourselves to others. Love in the context of relationships is not as dependable as our True Nature. Love can cause great joy and also great suffering. Unlike universal love, relationships can be as transitory as the emotions that drive them. Love as it relates to relationships can be fleeting. Knowing this, however, should compel us to work harder to make our relationships work, especially when children are involved.

Marriage and parenting are not easy endeavors, yet so many people jump into both without much thought or self-reflection. Many times, relationships test the emotional baggage and control patterns we harbor. The more mindful we are of ourselves and the more we trust in the space our True Nature gives us to grow and change; the more responsive we can be in relationships; thus increasing happiness and decreasing suffering. We all need to work at relationships and love. The second we stop working to make our relationships cohesive is the moment they tend to unravel. Failing relationships can have a deep impact on you, your partner, and especially the children you share. Likewise, an abusive or unbalanced relationship can facilitate suffering as well.

Relationships can be as complex as the challenges they tend to weave. Still, I see no reason why intimate relationships can't exist free of control patterns and drama. I do have one breakdown to share that I find effective.

Love in relationships can be reduced to three key elements:

1. **Emotions:** How we feel about each other.
2. **Ethics:** Whether we are good or bad for each other.
3. **Joy:** Whether or not we satisfy each other.

These three components determine the quality of our relationships. The elements relate to each other and blend, allowing us to better evaluate lasting relationships that involve more than just simple attraction. Relationships that work on all three levels are incredible sources of positive energy and connect us to higher levels of responsiveness within our lives. Finding the right partner in life can be challenging. Compatibility is like a puzzle. Finding the right pieces that fit in our lives can be difficult. I think one of the most important facets of a relationship is satisfaction. Satisfaction will enhance our ability to be open, aware, and loving partners, which brings balance to relationships and families.

A lasting relationship must be a dynamic push-and-pull. When you first meet someone, you may initially be enamored by his or her appearance and or personality. This is the infatuation phase, when everything is new, overwhelming, and intoxicating. Over time, infatuation dims and can either extinguish or transform into something greater—enduring love. Enduring love is accepting your partner for who they are. You understand your partner's weaknesses and you do not exploit them. You recognize your partner's strengths and you praise and support them. When your partner feels low, you are his or her primary source of encouragement. When you feel low, you seek out council and comfort from your partner. For love to last there is always this give-and-take. Unconditional love and enduring love means deep understanding, responsiveness, responsibility, and compromise.

Compromise and Communication

One of the most crucial ingredients to a lasting relationship is communication. Partners need to be able to share thoughts on the most intimate of levels. Effective communication is a two-way street: Partners must be able to speak and listen. They must be able to share thoughts and feelings without fear of potential backlash. As a responsive partner, it is important to remember that when arguments occur, trying to listen and understand where your partner is coming from, what he or she wants, is more productive than just immediately getting defensive or trying to drive your point across first. We also need to be more aware of the control patterns that arise in times of conflict and challenge with your partner. Nothing is more important because how you two handle the tough times will be the defining factor and ultimately the pass-or-fail in relationships. Be karmic in your words, actions and reactions, especially in times of adversity. Be aware of your intentions and blind reactions and be confident that are not born from the ego.

The shortest distance between two positions is intention. This is certainly true in relationships where you should always strive to be aware of what your partner's wants and needs are. Our actions as responsive partners should be grounded in desire and commitment; the sources of lasting love. Our choices, attitudes, and acts of kindness are valuable assets to our relationships. Your own intention to continually reach out and show your partner you really care sends out a series of positive actions. Remember, positive actions always create more positive reactions. This kind of focus and progress in your relationship guarantees a circle of positive energy around you, with you and your partner happy and balanced at the center.

Love and Energy

As individuals, we constantly regulate our own levels of energy in order to stay centered. Many times, however, we ignore our energy flow with our partner. A dominant partner most likely holds more energy than the recessive partner. Whatever the source of unbalance is between partners, the key to a healthy relationship rests in the ability to be equal—no matter what personality types you or your partner possess. This requires constant monitoring of personal needs and desires. It also requires dealing with any past issues or control patterns that may affect your ability to be truly open and loving.

With any actions we take, we first need to consider the repercussions our actions might have before we set them in motion. Understanding how our words, motives, and actions affect people will create responsiveness. In other words, always being mindful of what we do or say allows us to regulate the energy flow between ourselves and our partners so that we are creating a positive and nurturing atmosphere. This is true for all relationships, intimate or not. Every action we make in life creates a positive or negative reaction depending on our intention and how our action was received. Focusing on how our words and deeds affect those around us is a good way to break poor control patterns and eliminate unnecessary conflict. Negative actions can strip away our energy and our partner's energy. With this in mind, we can always re-think our wants and motives and determine the most productive and loving ways to handle situations.

In addition to being mindful of our energy flow, we can also simply build positive energy in our relationships by following these steps:

1. **Spend quality time together:** This can be time with friends, going to the movies, going to dinner, attending a sporting event, or cuddling while watching your favorite TV program. It is not the activity that is so important. Rather, it is the time spent together that strengthens the bond of companionship.

2. **Touch:** Even subtle gestures like a soft pat on the leg, a kiss on the cheek, or holding hands in public shows affection and a level of enduring love. It is a nonverbal way of showing that you care.

3. **Space:** We have talked at length about space and how it relates to us, the Universe, and our True Nature. With the need to spend

quality time together, also comes the need to spend some time apart. We all need space to be alone. It creates peace and creativity.

4. **Don't play games:** Toying with your partner's emotions is never productive. We all know our partner's weaknesses and how to push his or her buttons. Try to use mental triggers to help you avoid such responses, especially in times of conflict.

5. **Passion:** Find ways to rekindle the passion that was present when you first met. Get creative and make time to find those feelings of intense intimacy again.

6. **Communication:** Listen to what your partner has to say. Stop yourself when you feel it's more important to explain your side of the story. Instead, pause and find compassion for what your partner is saying or feeling. Then in a calm way, explain your perspective.

7. **Compliments:** Make it a habit, even if you have to push yourself, to compliment things you like and enjoy about your partner. We all get caught up in this thing called life. Now and then stop and compliment your partner when he or she least expects it.

8. **Turn off the gadgets:** iPads, tablets, and laptops have crept into our bedrooms. Nooks and Kindles also don't count as touching. Often excessive computer or smart-phone use becomes a replacement for something lacking in a relationship. If you or your partner starts to use gadgets non-stop, especially at bedtime, it is a sign that something needs to change.

9. **Control your anger:** This is important in relationships and especially with your children. Anger erodes peace and affects our decisions. Most anger is the product of blind reactions and only reinforces negative control patterns for you and your family.

10. **Get busy in bed:** We all have a primal need to connect at a more intimate level. With the busy lives we lead, sexual intimacy can often take a back seat to family and career. That is a mistake. Sex releases stress and continues to establish a warm, sensual bond between partners. Make time for love-making.

Create Mindful Gaps in your Day

So, maybe you had another stressful day in the office. So many of us take breaks from the stress and monotony of work to check personal email, maybe surf the internet, or perhaps head to the break-room for a snack. But is that really a break? Maybe some of you work so hard you forget to take breaks—the day travels by fast and furious and before you know it, it's time to go home and the "inbox" is still full!

If this sounds familiar, then try to incorporate "mindful gaps" in your day. We need gaps or meditative respites in our daily life to break up the controlled chaos that surrounds us. This includes the incessant thoughts that constantly stream through our heads. We need to create gaps in our thoughts that allow us to find some awareness of the present that is sandwiched between thoughts of the past and future: our ego faculties that are rooted many times in fear and fantasy.

For example, imagine stepping outside of the work place for a few moments:

Envision it is a cool spring afternoon outside your place of work; the wind is calm, the sun is out, and there is a handful of solitary clouds drifting by. You noticed new leaves regenerating to life on the bare branches of trees and the sound of birds frolicking around and about. In the far-off distance, the hum of a lawn mower; you feel the cool sensation of a peaceful breeze against your face as the maturing sun warms you from the west. The smell of spring is in the air—crisp and fresh. You breathe in deeply, inhaling positivity and exhaling the stress and negativity of the work day. For a moment, you feel present, centered and content. Now, imagine you experienced all of this in less than a minute. This is not a fantasy. This is being mindful of the present. Even if it was raining outside, your mindfulness of the present creates a gap in what was a busy day; maybe even a stressful day. Being mindful of your surroundings and internal thoughts and feelings builds space and clarity.

Gaps are important. A couple of minutes out of your day is well worth the trouble. Try to incorporate this type of mental exercise or meditation several times a day and things will look lighter and brighter during the workday.

Finding our Inward and Outward Balance

Wellness advocates talk of finding balance in our lives. This may include eating a balanced diet of fruit and veggies, a balance of exercise and even a balance of work verses play. I talk of meditation as a lifestyle tool, a journey in mindfulness. When you think of meditation you think of inner space, self-discovery, and enlightenment. We all have this quantifiable inward space: The realm of our mind, feelings and emotions, relaxation and anxiety, thoughts, memories and dreams, etc. What about outward space—our exterior surroundings? We always talk about finding a balance within our bodies but we rarely talk about balancing what is inside and what is outside as ONE. Take our homes and offices for example. When you walk into another person's personal space you can learn a lot about what is going in that person's life by how organized and neat they are—you can learn a lot about what is going on inside a person by their clothes, wall decorations, cleanliness, and mementos. Our exterior environments or our personal spaces are direct extensions of our inner realm, the mind. A person that is messy on the outside most likely has a cluttered mind on the inside; a mind with thoughts running rampant with fear and fantasy, past and future, rarely connected to the present. The opposite for the uncluttered minimalist can also be true; a mind of awareness and clarity, space and positive energy.

The art of happiness and wellness is finding a balance between our inner realm of mind and our outer realm of intent and action. It really should be a seamless division. It begins with space. Space within the mind can be boundless and relaxing, or closed off and anxious. Our living and working environments need to transcend the meditative goal of wellness, energy, and space. Our personal environments can be small, but they should be inviting, empowering and relaxing; a refuge, a sanctuary.

So, as we continue to be mindful and aware of what is going on inside our brains and body, let's also be equally aware of what is going on in our exterior environment. Be mindful of the clutter and how to better organize your belongings. Be mindful of what makes you happy and relaxed and carry that from your mind to your exterior world. Remember, clutter in the mind and in our surroundings suffocates us. Less is more and finding a balance both inward and outward is the evolutionary goal in self-discovery. Find that balance and you will find betterment.

The Heart and Mind

The heart and mind are often thought of as symbolically different ruling elements of our being. The heart is thought of as our center and it is literally found in our chest. The mind is most likely considered part of our brain and is of course found in our head. Symbolically speaking, the heart is the place where love and compassion reign. The mind is the space for analytical or occupational work. The heart is our True Nature where we find our courage and passion. The mind is where we find our egos, our self-esteem, survival instincts, and fear. Both spaces are required to focus and operate, but both are quite different in how they operate. It is easy to spot the differences between the heart and mind, but this type of thinking causes a rift in our being.

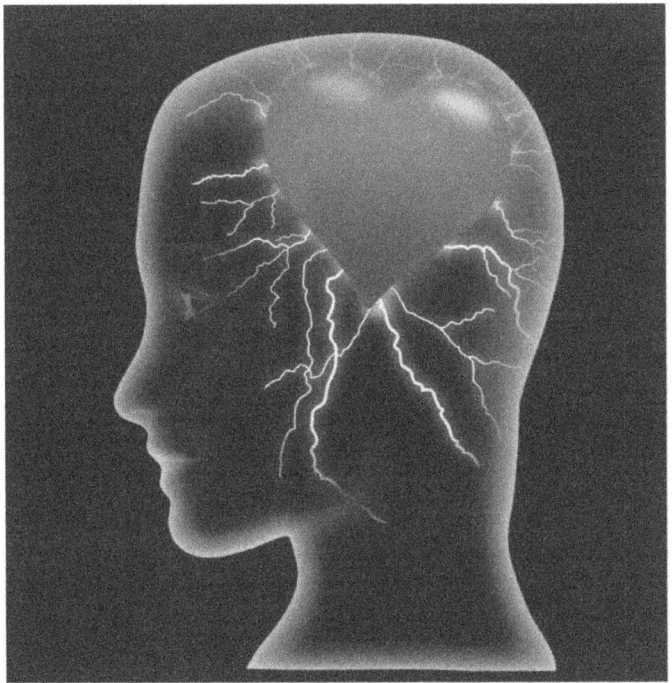

The heart and mind, the ego and True Nature: All are classic rifts within us that need awareness and eventually positive recourse

There tends to be a push-and-pull between the two forces which helps reinforce the wall between ego and True Nature and between the "material world" versus our "True Reality." For example, imagine that you live in a city you dislike because your job is there, but moving to the country has always been your dream. The city brings convenience and a good social life but you are older now and having land and space is your new-found dream. Your heart tells you that you're unhappy living where you are, but your mind tells you that you make good money at your job and you shouldn't give that up in this economy. It seems as if there are two voices within, bickering and presenting their own agenda. The question is which voice is right? It is a classic scenario where the heart and the mind engage in a push-pull that causes a divide in one's psyche. The common denominator for this phenomenon is internal strife and anxiety, which leads to suffering.

Instead of living with divided interests, we must strive to merge our heart and mind as one. When merged as one, the sum of the two is authentic empowerment that is centered and self-actualized. When we are centered in life, our heart-and-mind rift is mended, with both entities working together. Gone will be the rift; gone will be two voices; united will be your heart and mind working mutually toward self-evolution. One way to do this is to continually work to expand our connection to True Nature. We need to be mindful and connected to the present where space and clarity exist. Imagine something you enjoyed in the recent past, whether it's a vibrant sunrise or quality time with friends or family. Such actions will engage the heart and mind as one, feeding them positive energy. Notice how good you feel when your heart and mind are one. Think about how stress and sadness make you feel disconnected from this joy. It is so easy in our busy, chaotic lives to forget the things that really make us happy. Instead of always focusing on what needs to be done next or the full inbox at work, try to focus more on what makes you happy right now. Make time for the things that give you peace. This will reconnect the heart and the mind.

We all have obligations we can't ignore, but we must find a compromise between our feelings of responsibility and bliss. We all have to be responsible and pay the bills. That is the mind talking, and it isn't foolish talk. It's methodical and practical. We must listen to it, but we must also understand that it isn't the complete picture. We can still work and battle the inbox, but we can engage our hearts simultaneously by always connecting to our sources of joy and spending a little bit of time even in the work day meditating on them.

Furthermore, we must not lose sight that the heart-and-mind merger creates a boundless creative force in our lives that mirrors the essence of True Nature. When you are mindful of the present, centered, and happy, you feel incredibly open and aware. This feeling is boundless, and for a few fleeting moments, you may even feel like anything is possible. These feelings of hope and possibility are the essence of enlightenment. By becoming more vigilant in focusing on our sources of happiness, we become more steadfast in our journey towards awareness and clarity. Your quality of life will improve, as you will become more conscious of what makes you happy and what stresses you out. You will become more present in your surroundings and more aware of their effect on you. Through this ongoing exercise in expanding your mindfulness, the heart-and-mind rift will heal and you will feel whole and self-actualized.

Meditation Session

In your next meditation, let your mind focus on a situation or a dependency that you struggle with. It can be food, smoking, the need for attention, or even a substance addiction. Recall our recent discussions of the rift between the heart and the mind. In any situation of suffering or dependency, this classic rift is at play: Our heart tells us we are heading down a path of suffering and destruction, but our ego-driven mind will formulate excuses and reasons for us to stay on that path and not change. Born from the mind, our egos can sound very analytical and convincing. We feel guilt and remorse for knowing we are allowing this destruction, but because of our false-perceptions at play, the guilt does not awaken us to change. Instead, it further feeds the monster in our minds that destroys our self-worth and weakens our resolve to improve our lives. When you consider the situation or dependency causing you suffering, can you sense this rift between your heart and mind? Can you hear what you heart says to you versus what your mind speaks? Can you feel the tug of war between ego and your True Nature?

Addiction and suffering are unnecessary bi-products of the ego, low self-esteem, and fear. In this meditation, breathe in the space and strength you need to separate yourself from this situation that binds you. This can be any situation that causes suffering in your life. Listen to what your heart tells you. Give that voice more volume than the ego-governed mind. Really feel the heart-mind rift and know that tension and struggle is your trigger to do the right thing. Once you release yourself from this situation or dependency that causes you pain, you will suffer less. You will start to take actions to work against this destructive behavior. In this meditation, make the space in your mind for a life that is better, free of attachments and cravings.

Let's focus on a new mantra. "Breathe in positive energy and strength; breathe out false-self and dependency."

Daily Life Practice

In Buddhist philosophy, there are edicts known as the Four Noble Truths:

1. The existence of suffering
2. The origin of suffering
3. The end of suffering
4. The path to the end of suffering

In this daily life practice, acknowledge that suffering appears to be intrinsic to life; especially when the ego is unknowingly involved in daily rituals. It is a fact of existence and will be present in our lives until we achieve full enlightenment. Try to determine the root of your suffering. It may be an event in your past, a present control pattern, or both. Make a vow to yourself to end this suffering. Know in your heart that the less you suffer, the happier and more evolved you will be. After you make this vow to yourself, devise a plan to rid yourself of this suffering. Determine your wants and set your intentions to match them. Deploy mental triggers to become more aware of the actions and thoughts that lead you to suffering instead of happiness. Further, come up with steps to lead a healthier life and make small daily changes to remind yourself that dedication and diligence will bring you great rewards. Eating better, meditation, and learning to love better are examples of how we can enrich our daily existence.

If you're at a loss to start, follow these simple steps to perpetuate a healthier and more positive existence:

1. **Find space:** Have openness and space for the events of daily life. Settle into the vastness of your mind and the Universe and how both relate to your True Nature.
2. **Wake up every day in a peaceful mood:** Try to wake up without annoying alarm clocks. Give yourself more time to wake up and get ready for what should be a good day. Avoid feeling rushed or

stressed. Tell yourself each day before getting out of bed that today is going to be good.

3. **Control your breathing:** Learn to breathe in positive energy and breathe out stress and worry. Take time during the day to focus on deep, long breathes in and out and you will feel more relaxed and peaceful. Try it any time you feel stressed or anxious.

4. **Live with an open mind:** Adopt an unbiased approach to learning and love. Make your own conclusions and decisions following your own careful reasoning. Review those ideas and opinions left in your mind from childhood influences and social immersion, and keep only those that are productive to you today. Begin to see life through your own eyes and not the eyes of others.

5. **Find faith in something positive:** Make your own researched opinions about God and creation and always be open to changing your opinions as you gain more and more knowledge.

6. **Be aware of control patterns:** Review your actions in life and determine if they are genuine or if they are determined by negative control patterns you harbor. Recognize negative control patterns before you act, and change the sequence of events by creating new positive actions to replace old hard-wired behaviors.

7. **Live with compassion and live without hate:** Hate is a mental cancer that will eat you alive from the inside. If someone is causing you grief, try to understand why instead of just hating them. Try to feel compassion for this person. Compassion will release your negative feelings and will allow you to think clearly in order to handle the situation more constructively.

8. **Appreciate nature:** Take time each day to appreciate something beautiful in nature. The natural beauty in life is God's power. Focusing on it for just a few seconds will bring peace and renewed energy levels.

9. **Think positive:** Try replacing negative thoughts with positive ones. Focusing on positive thinking will create a new dynamism that will manifest positive reactions.

10. **Meditation:** A light form of meditation may involve simply controlling your breathing and thinking of the positives in your life. A deeper form may take you into your subconscious and align your body with your True Nature.

11. **Appreciate others:** It is important to stop what we are doing and then focus on the people around us who influence our lives in

positive ways. It is also important for us to tell these people that we appreciate them.

12. **Exhibit good karma:** Our world is based on cause and effect. We live in a revolving Universe of matter and energy. Positive and negative actions we create will eventually return to us as equal energy. Why not act positively?

13. **Stay centered:** Be mindful of when you are stressed or having a bad day. This awareness should be a trigger for change. When all possible, root your thoughts in the present, away from past and future; fear and fantasy. This will center our energy. When centered, we are aligned with our True Nature.

14. **Go to bed in a peaceful mood:** Relive the high points of your day before falling asleep. Remember the people who made a positive impression on you. Have compassion for those who affected you negatively. Try not to focus on what needs to be done tomorrow. Focus on the great day you had today.

15. **Be responsive:** Be aware and mindful of your thoughts and your surroundings. Always be connected to your True Nature. Having sensitivity to our environment breeds wisdom and enlightenment.

Meditation Revisited

Have I mentioned this enough? We talked extensively about meditation in the Second Mandala. Meditation is a valuable tool in being mindful of the present moment and finding a connection to True Nature. Don't give up on your meditation practice just because you feel you can't commit twenty minutes each day. Find different ways to focus and become cognitive of the constant stream of thoughts and emotions that rush through your mind. There are countless ways to be mindful: You can turn a walk with the dog, a commute to work, a coffee break, or a daily swim into a meditation. Even creating small gaps of mindfulness throughout the day and especially at work are forms of meditation. If only for a few minutes, any form of meditation will have lasting effects on your overall wellness. Take some time during more restful moments you already have in your day to become more aware of your breathing. Find the space and awareness to connect your breath with your mind and body. Continue to be mindful of how you feel at the present moment. Are your thoughts positive, negative, or neutral in their energy source? Your ego may intervene and tell you that you don't have time for such trivial concerns, but nothing could be further from the truth.

I still strongly recommend making time for a more formal meditative session, but go ahead and start small; it is fine to limit your expectations. The definition of meditation is simply being mindful of your thoughts and finding awareness of the present. Further, each meditative session will be different than the last and some will seem more productive than others—still, even what you might think is an unproductive meditation is still meditation. Remember, even if your mind is awash with thoughts and you find it difficult to focus on a meditative strategy, this is to be considered part of the meditation. This is what meditation is—any effort to be mindful is a meditative effort. Once you start to see the positive changes with taking five minutes out of the day to focus on your breath, you might be inspired to carve out more time to increase the positive changes. Meditation takes diligence, but you will soon see positive transformations. Even if you don't feel like you're making a difference at first, keep in mind that just making the effort to be more mindful is enough.

The Seventh Mandala

The Seventh Mandala builds a strong foundation of support and wellness as we continue our journey toward self-actualization. By living healthy lives, eating well, and exercising, we create immediate positive results. Love for life and love for others reinforces positive physical and mental health. Living in moderation equips us with the ability to be aware of our bad habits and get into routines of healthy living. Moderation means we understand our needs versus just our wants and desires. All of these practices in the Seventh Mandala are easy to adopt and they pave the way toward wellness and happiness and away from the ego and suffering. Please remember that every positive experience you have further aligns your body with your True Nature. The Seventh Mandala provides lists and outlines for several experiences and activities you can have that are positive. You don't need to wait for good things to happen. You can make them happen yourself.

Seventh Mandala Exit Strategy

- Have awareness for the various modes of positive energy found in our daily life from nature, wellness, to love.
- Find a balance in life with moderation and work to break the chains of addiction (both passive and acute) that cause us to needlessly suffer.
- Focus and heal your heart-and-mind rift.
- Meditate on what in life makes you suffer. Be aware that addiction and suffering are born from the ego. Turn toward more positive elements and work to change your lifestyles. Be mindful of the abrasive qualities associated with doing the right thing.
- Mantra: "Breathe in positive energy and strength, breathe out false-self and dependency."

- Daily Life Practice: Acknowledge the Four Noble truths as a path to understanding suffering and connect to your True Nature as a solution to ending suffering.

The Eighth Mandala

Karma and Positive Energy

The Eighth Mandala

The first seven Mandalas make up the foundation vital to the pursuit of truth and personal self-discovery. These Mandalas affirm and analyze the past so that positive, self-directed decisions can be made for the future. As we move on to the Eighth Mandala, we shift our focus from the internal to more of the external and explore the Buddhist philosophy that offers the concept that one is not fully enlightened and free from suffering until the world is at peace. This chapter encourages a broader understanding of the world we live in and encourages us to study the energies that surround and connect us.

Karma

I have referenced the concept of karma several times in our journey forward to betterment. Now let's take a closer look at what karma is and what it means in a Responsive Universe. In Buddhist and Hindu teachings, the law of karma states that for every event that occurs, other events will follow. These subsequent events are the direct result of the first event and will be pleasant or unpleasant depending on the first event. Our actions, whether good or bad, cause ripples in the web of life, much like a stone tossed in a calm pond. The ripples of water caused by the tossed stone are forces of energy reverberating outward in all directions. The ripples do not die out when they reach the edge of the pond. On the contrary, they bounce back to the source. Similarly, karma explains that an action brings inevitable results. Religious overtones aside, karma is simply a law of cause and effect and can be seen as a principle of reward based on good intentions and deeds. Karma emphasizes a maintained pattern of behavior based on one's intrinsic sense of right and wrong and desire to be responsible for one's own actions. Unlike religions where sins or wrongdoing can be forgiven or admonished, karma is true justice. There is no recourse with karmic energy—once an action or ripple of energy is created, nothing can stop the impending sequence of events. No matter what, any action will be following by other related events. This law of action and consequences transcends all creeds and culture—it is inescapable.

"Karma is not something complicated or philosophical. Karma means watching your body, watching your mouth, and watching your mind. Trying to keep these three doors as pure as possible is the practice of karma".

Lama Thubten Yeshe

The Responsive Universe

Also, unlike religions that require faith in fables and ancient parables, the concept of karma displays evidence as an actual law of nature. One such strain of evidence comes from the study of brain chemistry as it relates to emotions. The human body is a highly organized population of approximately 50 trillion cells. Scientific evidence proves that actual human emotions, like anger and love, cause various unique chemical reactions in the brain. You can imagine our emotions creating metaphorical weather patterns that affect our cells—enlightenment and bliss being the perfect climate for life, and anger and fear being a storm of negativity. The health and wellness of one's cells depends on their emotional climate. One determines their emotional climate by his or her actions. More positive actions in life create brain chemicals geared toward pleasure and happiness, a process which can be described as "brain chemical karma." Conversely, negative actions can create internal suffering.

Popular theories in applied sciences such as the Torsion Field Theory also support the law of karma in nature. The Torsion Field Theory, conceived in the 1980s by Soviet physicists, asserts that within physics, a field is an assignment of quantity within each point of space-time. A torsion field includes any variable that describes rotation. A well-studied quantum phenomenon called spin-spin interaction suggests that subatomic particles called neutrinos do not carry mass or energy but only information as they are transmitted across space. Torsion field theories echo the 19th century notion of "Universal Ether" or "Aether." Aether is a term used to describe the medium for the propagation of light and energy. It has mythological origins, and ancient philosophers such as Plato and Aristotle described it as a Fifth Element. The concept of Aether enables theorists to use quantum mechanics to describe an information-energy field of interconnections, signals, events, and processes. Information garnered from actions in life can be carried across these paths of information and light as karmic energy in the form of weak electromagnetic pulses.

Newton's Third Law of Motion, which states that for every action, there is an equal and opposite reaction, gives more widely accepted scientific proof that karma exists as a law of nature. Likewise, sub-atomic physics explains that a simple human action creates an invisible quantum motion of force at a microscopic level and is met by further reactions, a direct result of the first event. These quantum forces in motion carry positive and negative actions and reactions through our conscious and subconscious worlds. Intentions and feelings rotate across space like neutrinos, carrying information that might not directly interact with matter, but can be generated and detected easily. Thus positive and negative actions can be equated with energy that is always in motion. Einstein described the world as a place of matter and form dictated by a quantum field of energy that comprises everything. All matter, whether as enormous as a red giant star or as minute as a single atom, has invisible but perceptible energy pulsing through it. As discussed earlier, scientific experiments reveal startling results when elementary particles are broken down and observed, revealing perceptible patterns of energy. Even the act of observation itself can alter the results, as if elementary particles are influenced by the expectations of the observer.

The point being, science proves that even thoughts themselves have vibrations that spin out into the invisible web of energy that connects us all, and medical studies show that even small acts of kindness have profound positive effects on mental and physical well being. All of these studies, laws, and theories lead us to understand that karma drives energy (good or bad) in this Responsive Universe. Still, people often have a philosophical misunderstanding of karma. Karma isn't just a system of punishment and reward but an exchange of energy between conscious entities. If a person physically hurts someone, he or she will not necessarily be greeted by a reaction of suddenly having their arm broken by the other. Much like that stone cast in the water, there is not just one ripple reverberating outwards from an action, but many ripples. It is impossible to pinpoint the exact time or actual event in regard to a karmic reaction. Plus, reactions can take many forms and variables. For example, the reaction of a negative karmic event could be enduring subsequent bad luck, or it could be living with the guilt or depression caused by one's negative action. The important thing to remember is that our intentions and actions alter and affect the climate of the energy field around us at all times. Whether karma is born from the chemical reactions of our brains, a sub-atomic life force, or quantum physics, it is prudent to be aware of one's actions because they will affect others, and your actions will inevitably come back to affect you.

There is some debate as to how negative karma or negative energy exists in an otherwise positive Responsive Universe. Unfortunately, this is where facts stop and conjecture begins. I firmly believe that negativity is a human invention (much like the concept of Hell) and does not exist in the Universe beyond our planet. Still, it is rather hard to fathom us as separate from the Universe. We are in fact products of the Cosmos but it is our conscious thought that created the existence of negative energy or bad karma here on Earth. Could karma exist elsewhere in the Cosmos? Anything is possible in a Responsive Universe, but I would surmise that negativity is a rare anomaly in the vastness of space and time. I find it interesting that negativity is such a driving force on our small, impressible planet. Still, positivity seems to be the backbone of instinctual, conscious energy. Even death itself is not negative; in fact the essence of death may very well be the most under-rated and beautiful energy exchange yet to be experienced in life. Yet, negative energy does exist here on Earth. It is an energy entirely created by humans alone. Born from the ego and false-self, it is a force entirely wielded by humans alone. Negative energy has no purpose within the Absolute Universe. It can only thrive on our planet where our thoughts and actions carry energy that colors and even alters space-time. Just think: Unlike negative energy that is confined to our planet as an entirely human notion and invention, positive energy is a life source that thrives everywhere we perceive and even everywhere we can only imagine: Here on Earth, through the Cosmos, and even in the afterlife. It makes you wonder why anyone would choose to act according to negative energy, which literally limits our ability to self-evolve; when you can choose to act according to a positive energy that is literally boundless as it is sublime.

Positive Energy

Modern science suggests that the subconscious brain is capable of processing 20,000,000 environmental stimuli per second. Our conscious brain, on the other hand, struggles with as few as 40 processes per second. It isn't a huge leap to see why, with the incredible processing power of the subconscious mind, so many people experience good results from techniques of positive thinking like meditation and prayer. In the Responsive Universe, the power of positive thinking comes from connecting to our True Nature, our intrinsic and immortal connection with humanity and the Cosmos, from which energy and all forms arise. With an open mind, we have the ability to take in information and channel it through the millions of neurons within our brains. Then, within this Responsive Universe, we can take this a step further—positive thinking becomes positive energy, as the information we take in and the information we subsequently project is all connected in the Universe's vast electromagnetic energy field that links all matter, tangible and intangible.

Over the centuries, the concept of positive energy has taken many names across cultures, including the Japanese Ki, the Chinese Chi, the Indian Prana, and the Greek Aether. All of these names describe the same concept: The life-process or flow of energy that sustains living beings and our subsequent environment. Recall in the Third Mandala, we observed that the Universe is an expanding bundle of energy that continually forms new matter from old matter. The stars in the night sky die and exhale tired gases to form new nebulae, the birthplace of new stars. Similarly, life and death share a revolving door in cosmological terms. Positive energy is based on this same circular premise or Mandala. The actions and thoughts we put out into the world will be met with actions and thoughts that are the direct result of our original actions, and so forth, in a continual circular pattern with no end. When we channel our thoughts through positive thinking, we produce energy capable of causing positive reactions or manifestations that ripple through our interconnected surroundings, as seen and proven with the quantum mechanical laws of the Universe.

The point to this explanation of energy is simple. We are all connected to each other through a matrix of energy and matter. Every action we make, word we speak, and intention we project, creates an energy that not only affects this life matrix, but also creates an energy response that returns to us in some form. Simple daily actions may seem inconsequential, but when you add up positive actions and equate that with energy, there is a definite trend or shift in our wellness to be appreciated, especially over the long term. The same can be said for negative energy. Those that live life through ego, domination, and fear will suffer as a result.

We are led again to a discussion of an afterlife. After all, we now understand that energy cannot be destroyed when our mortal bodies die. Even in the violent and ever-changing event-horizons of black holes where even light cannot escape; basic information remains intact based on new contemporary theories in astrophysics. Doesn't it make sense to leave a positive energy footprint here in the mortal world before we join the hereafter? We may not fully comprehend life after death, but anchoring ourselves to positivity and True Nature seems instinctively the evolutionary path. With such amazing gifts comes a great responsibility to live well and be kind to people. As individuals with our own needs, wants and desires, you and I will never cease to suffer until the collective world joins in the same wellness and contentment. This may seem like an impossible endeavor, but the premise here is not to take the weight of the world's problems on your own shoulders but understand that humanity is connected at levels so intricate and multifaceted that we need join together in commonality instead of being divided by petty differences. We are all connected in a symbiotic relationship and true enlightenment will never be self-actualized until this notion of compassion and commonality is appreciated on a global scale. The simplicity of this idea—that positivity breeds positivity in an endless circle that binds us all—is truly the gift of enlightenment.

Nyams

"Nyams" is a term in Tibetan Buddhist psychology that describes a thunderbolt of enlightenment. It is a feeling of intense instinctual energy, a so-called fit of brilliance, or what Oprah Winfrey once described as an "Aha!" moment. In a dream-state, the dreamer can have a powerful vision he or she remembers vividly. Experiencing a Nyams while awake, however, is much more powerful. In order to achieve a state of being where you can tap into this intense instinctual energy, you must focus on keeping your thoughts and energy centered on the present and the positive, away from memories or the past or projections into the future that are typically rooted in ego, fear, and fantasy. Meditation is a very beneficial tool in focusing one's thoughts and finding space in the mind and body to feel these charged pulses of energy. This energy reminds us what true self-actualization and enlightenment must feel like. At times, a Nyams may come in the form of a revelation or wisdom you hear from your inner voice. Other times, it may just be a feeling; a feeling of warmth and bliss for no apparent reason—just a moment of perfect contentment, a gaping smile for no reason. Experiencing any of these feelings or emotions is a good sign that you are on your path to self-discovery. You are projecting positive energy into the Universe and receiving it back in its most fulfilling form. Be mindful of these feelings and also the source of such feelings. Imagine feeling like this more often!

Energy Vortexes

When I describe True Nature, it can be construed that this energy comes from within. This is a bit misleading because there really is no boundary in regard to our True Nature. Further, the mind and the Universe are all unified with our True Nature in a complex tapestry of energy, celestial wisdom and instinct. Taking it a step further, there are elements of our environment here on Earth that hold or give off unusually high levels of energy. Maybe you have heard of Sedona's Vortex? There are special places, especially in nature, that stimulate sensitivity thus exceeding our basic senses. There is a meta-physical quality to such enhanced energy sites. People speak of these places as being vortexes that allow one to connect to a higher level of senses and actually be moved or invigorated by the mysterious energies that surround us. These invisible energies are the basis of quantum physics. As you now understand, quantum physics describes an energy field in which everything is connected. There are high and low levels of energy present throughout the Universe and here on Earth. We as humans are interconnected with this energy and the more mindful we are in the present moment, beyond ego, the more awareness we achieve; with this, a higher level of wisdom and responsiveness is actualized.

Yes, there are famous energy vortexes like "Bell Rock" found near Sedona. The Pyramids of Egypt, Manchu Picchu, even old nostalgic churches and temples can hold higher levels of energy. And we can find places of higher energy everywhere, including near our homes. Further, as unique individuals with our own unique vibration, we all connect and perceive energy differently. What might be a powerful and healing place for one person could be nothing special for another person. And then there are peripheral energy sources like music, meditation, or simply a pleasant conversation with an empowering person. Love and compassion are great sources of energy as well. So, the concept of an energy vortex is loosely defined. Nature is a guaranteed source, but we can find energy and empowerment everywhere. One just needs to be mindful of what makes them relaxed, happy, and empowered, and then the key is to visit these special places or experiences as much as possible.

The Cathedral Vortex in Sedona, AZ

The Responsive Universe

All sorts of spaces can "speak" to us, whether they are the dusty red canyons and ridges of the American Southwest, inspiring ocean coastlines, the hustle and bustle of big cities, or the boundless essence of an aware and meditative mind.

"...The human perception of this energy first begins with a heightened sensitivity to beauty."

James Redfield

No matter where we feel great sources of energy, the common denominator for humanity is that we are all products of the Universe. We are all connected by vibrating waves of quantum energy. Even though we still can't solve all the mysteries of the Universe, we can still revel in its beauty and immensity. Sometimes knowing we are a part of this magnificent design is enough. We can feel the beauty of nature and cityscapes as it relates to our True Nature—a connection to something so grand and sublime that sometimes words can't describe, but our feelings and emotions can comprehend with reverence. Whether you connect to natural, unadulterated energy in your back yard or while backpacking the Rocky Mountains, being present within an energy vortex lets us know that we are part of something so vast and amazing, it can overwhelm the mind and bring peace all within the same instant. Just as there is great energy in geographical marvels, there is great energy inside each one of us. We can tap into and wield this energy through compassion, karma, and mindfulness.

The Maroon Bells near Aspen Colorado incorporates the rugged beauty of nature with a quality of space that breeds reverence

One great thing about finding inspirational spaces is that we can remember them or return to them when we lose hold of the energy source that exists inside ourselves. It is worth reiterating that this energy technically never leaves us. It is simply obscured by ego and the challenges and conflicts of life. These energy vortexes remind us of our connection to the Universe and our part within the Cosmos. At those times in our lives when ego and false perceptions muddle our True Nature, the amazing energy of places like Sedona can restore our sense of clarity. Even at those times in our lives when we are focused and clear, energy vortexes can help us connect with more vigor and intensity. The challenge for us all is to find spaces outside and also inside ourselves that are continual sources of boundless positive energy.

Bio-Energy Therapy

Just as nature and energy vortexes speak to us through their silence, healing energy also surrounds us. There are many forms of bio-energy healing therapies. Reiki is probably one of most well-known remedies. Reiki is Japanese for spiritually-guided life-energy.

Energy healing is based on the fact that humans are very energetic organisms. We create heat, give off light, generate electricity, and even have a measurable magnetic field. According to the principles of quantum physics, we are actually energy beings that occupy a physical space. Popular theories in applied sciences such as the Torsion Field Theory support the concept of bio-energy in nature. Scientifically, bio-energy healers are creating permutations in the vacuum or aether or zero-point-field via torsion fields, which in turn changes the characteristics of the source mass. It has been proven that conscious intent causes heightened electromagnetic fields in the surrounding of the practitioners hands, thus creating an alteration in the torsion field and creates new annihilation/energy opportunities for the source. M. Sue Benford, R.N., M.A., states: "The acceptance and appreciation of torsion fields, with their influencing spin characteristics both in defining and refining matter, opens a new perspective of scientific exploration into psi-phenomena. Possibly, we can conclude that life, and even mind, may be a manifestation of the constant, albeit subtle, interaction of the wave packets classically known as 'matter' with the underlying physically real Vacuum field."

We now understand that the body and surrounding aura emit energy and that human hands harness much of the energy. We know of the existence of the human body's electromagnetic energy field because high tech equipment, such as a SQUID (Superconducting Quantum Interference Device), EMG, EKG, and EEGs have been used to measure these extremely weak signals. These devices not only detect the presence of such energies, but can show how the laying on of hands (therapeutic touch), and other healing methods such as and Qi (which stands for Vital Force), can actually alter the subtle energy field of a subject.

Another fascinating aspect of the human hand is the power of its magnetism, in comparison to other major body parts. In 1963, researchers at Syracuse University reported the first measurements of the magnetic field of the human heart, just a millionth the strength of the earth's magnetic field. In 1971, a SQUID was used to measure the magnetic field of the brain which was 100 times weaker than the heart. Finally, the magnetic field between the hands of healers was measured as 1 milligauss. This is less than 1% the strength of Earth's magnetic field, but 1000 times as strong as the heart.

In more recent studies using a more modern device, a Triaxial ELF (Extra-Low-Frequency) Magnetic Field Meter to measure changes in magnetic fields, several successful studies were conducted from 2004-2006 by M.

Connor, G. Tau, and G. Schwartz, in Tucson. The study, titled, "Oscillation of Amplitude as Measured by an Extra Low Frequency Magnetic Field Meter as a Physical Measure of Intentionality" involved Energy Healers from several different regions and schools of thought. The studies not only showed remarkable increases in bio-energy but that Energy Medicine Practitioners can produce increased and decreased biophoton emission in plants. The fact that bio-energy is not just reserved for humans means healing energy can be used on animals and any other life forms.

A bio-energy healer does not use his/her own energy but rather directs bio-energy, which contains all the information your body needs to heal itself. The therapist directs the energy to the part of the body where it is needed, or takes the excess energy away from the part where there is too much energy. In other words, the therapist supplies the body with the information, contained in the bio-energy, which is necessary for proper functioning of the immune system, and the body begins to heal.

Bio-energy healing coupled with meditation is a powerful combination that can be used to heal, center and solicit a higher level of awareness within. With the proper training, anyone can learn to heal using bio-energy. All that is needed is the intent and confidence to heal; the quantum Universe takes care of the rest.

Meditation Session

Walking Meditation

As I stated earlier, you can meditate anytime and anywhere. I can't emphasize this enough: Meditation is any type of mindfulness where you are centering your energy and thoughts in the present. This means you are not thinking about the past or the future, your fears, and or your fantasies. It means you are not letting your mind run rampant with random thought trails. Instead, you are rooted completely in the present moment. What is happening right now…? and now… and now…?

That is meditation and yes it can be that simple. It's not that simple, though, is it? Keeping your thoughts centered in the present takes continued diligence and perseverance. Walking meditations (or even bike-riding meditations) are a great way to remain centered in the moment while being mobile and aware of outside stimulus. The biggest difference between a formal sitting meditation session and a walking meditation is that your eyes obviously need to be open while walking and you are also taking in outside stimulus whereas in a formal sit down meditation you are taking in and processing mostly inside stimulus.

A sitting meditation allows you to settle into mind and body completely, connecting the out-breath with energy and awareness. It allows you to stretch those gaps between thoughts so that inner wisdom can well up from within. A walking meditation draws from the same principles of inner wisdom but also incorporates the outside world. Especially in nature, there is a blend of inner tranquility with the tranquility and energy of our natural outside environment. Yes, you have to watch where you are going so you do not trip or run into something, but there is the added mindfulness of outside stimulus like wind and sun against your face, perhaps bare feet in the sand or grass, the visual interest of light glistening off of dew in the morning or a vibrant sunset to the west. There is an added benefit to being fully present with mind and body and also connected to the environment around you. A bridge is crossed between inward and outward qualities of mindfulness, which grounds you to your physical environment.

Make time to take a walk or bike ride in a local nature preserve or park, preferably away from scores of people. Less people can mean fewer distractions. Get lost in nature and your outside environment. Look up and be aware of the sky. Look down and be aware of the detail before you. Look out over the horizon and value the space around you and within you. Find silence in nature and your natural environment. Instead of random thoughts driving your mind, let your outer and inner environment drive the experience. Every time your thoughts stray, refocus on an element of nature.

For a new mantra repeat: "Breathe in positive energy, breathe out good karma and credibility."

Daily Life Practice

During a walking meditation, fears, worries, and anxieties can surface as errant thoughts draw your attention away from the present. These might be just passive fears or anxieties but these wayward thoughts are taking your awareness away from the present. This is totally normal and some sessions will be more challenging than others. Thoughts may include how you are going to pay the rent or mortgage next month. Maybe you need new tires on the car. Maybe you forgot to mail that thank-you letter to your friend. Yes, these are all important things, but not in this moment. Not right now. Such worries will simply repeat themselves needlessly in your mind. Be mindful of unnecessary thoughts replaying in your mind. While outside, try this simple daily life practice during any meditative respite marred by thoughts of worry and anxiety: As a negative or worrisome thought arises in the mind, visually imagine yourself pinching the thought with your fingers and actually placing it on a tree in the far-off distance. I know, a bit strange but give it a try. That rent or mortgage is not going to get paid right now. Get creative, and place that concern on the peak of a house in the distance. Put the worry of future car repairs on that car moving away from you in the distance. Those unfinished tasks that you will undoubtedly complete later; for now, attach them to that cloud floating high above your head. Be mindful that there is so much space inward and outward. Place those worries, anxieties, and fears away from you. These are symbolic gestures that will immediately create breathing space within your environment. See the space around you and visualize the space within you. Notice how when you make space for a worry it dissolves temporarily. Where did it go? Remember you can control your own space and thus your own stress levels. Be mindful that you are always in control and your only focus right now is the present; thus stretching those gaps between thoughts to allow inner wisdom to well from your True Nature.

The Circle Theory

We have discussed centering our thoughts in the present, beyond ego and false-self. What does it really mean to center ourselves? We now understand our intrinsic connection to the quantum energy force that flows through the Universe. It is a positive flow of power that exists everywhere, pulsing through the Cosmos and creating new life. We can manifest our own positive reactions through positive thoughts and actions (karma), thus creating a new dynamism that echoes through our lives. This dynamism helps us become centered so that we can recognize and connect to our True Nature. A helpful model to understanding this premise is something I call "The Circle Theory."

The Circle Theory

EGO

NEGATIVITY — HATE

ANGER — Enlightenment and Self Actualization — JEALOUSY

ANXIETY — GREED

FEAR

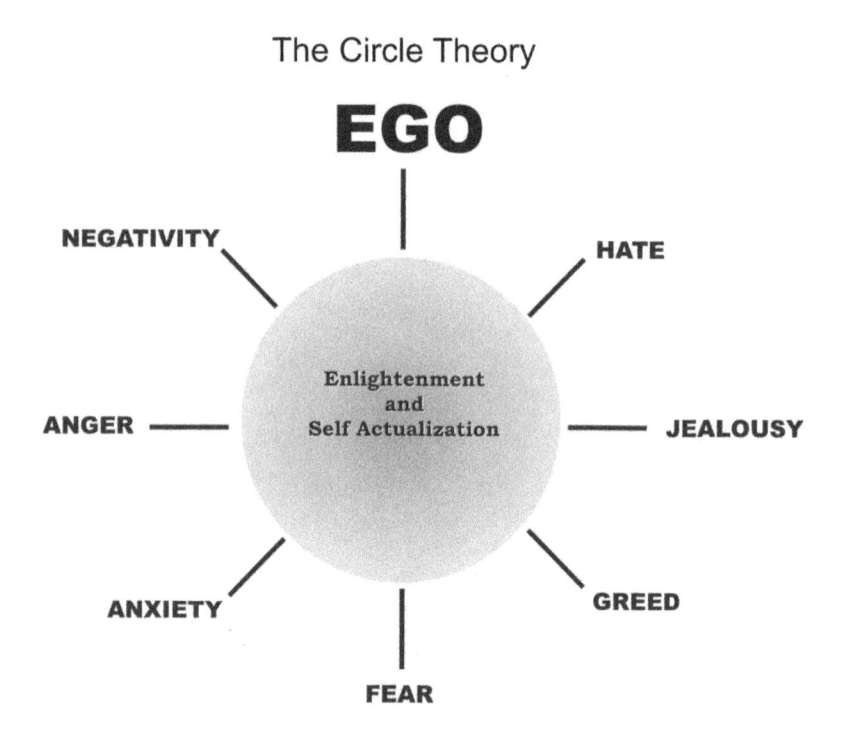

Imagine a circle or sphere of energy. Now imagine quantum energy as being the most powerful right in the center or core of that orb. Next imagine yourself in the center of that sphere or circle. When we are centered, or self-actualized, we can attain new knowledge because our minds are spacious, aware, and receptive. Centered, we are able to think for ourselves and successfully weed through societal conformity to be a true individual with empowering thoughts we call our own. Centered, we have an intimate faith in God as it relates to the Universe. We believe in our own theological principles based on our own well-thought life conclusions. Centered, we understand our childhood and upbringing, so that when we create new actions in life, we are not basing them on earlier negative models of behavior and control patterns. Centered, we are able to tap into all sources of positive energy around us, creating a feeling of bliss and even euphoria. By being centered in our energy and actions we are evolving socially and spiritually. Through this self-discovery we are adding credibility and wellness to our lives; thus setting a positive example for others to observe.

On the outside of the circle are the ills waiting in the shadows to knock you off your center. These ills include low self-esteem, anxiety, addiction, fear, hate, greed, jealousy, and conflict. These ills may sound familiar—they are common attributes of our ego. As we wrestle with daily life, challenges repeatedly confront us, whether they are relationship frustrations, conflicts with co-workers, or credit card debt. The list can be endless. Every negative issue pulls you away from your center and drags you closer to the edge where chaos and mediocrity rule. The edge of the circle contains the least amount of energy. It is at the edge where one's quality of life dwindles and suffers. Sadly, within a world wrought with war, famine, and big-money corporations controlling our fuel, food, and spirituality many people live on the edge of the circle looking in. This type of environment is stagnant and humans are unable to evolve socially and spiritually. Remaining centered is a constant journey that does not end until we exhale our last mortal breath. We must always be conscious of where we are in our circle of energy and we must always be striving to be at the center. Though challenging at times, working towards being centered is a rewarding journey. It is a great way to stay mindful of our emotions and surroundings to make sure the energy we are taking in and expelling is positive.

To be centered is to feel relaxed, confident, and mindful of the present. At times, it requires all of us to stop what we are doing for a moment and become aware of where we are in our circle. Throughout the day, ask yourself, "Am I centered?" There is a need to create gaps in our daily life where we can slow the controlled chaos, silence the incessant hum of society, and simply take a deep breath. It means focusing on something that comforts and relaxes us, to allow our bodies to accept positive energy from our surroundings. Try focusing on an energy vortex, even one near your home or place of employment. Focus on a particular tree or far-off hill, or maybe on a cloud in the sky. Perhaps a smell you love, perhaps the salty air of the ocean or the earthly scent from a nearby field or forest. Focus on a soothing melody or the memory of a special moment you had with someone. Focus on something that evokes peace and tranquility, space and clarity. Energy comes in many forms and from many sources. The idea is to take the energy from this source and let it course through your mind and body. Regulate your breathing so that you inhale the energy and exhale all the negativity pulling you from your center. Try this several times a day for just a few seconds, and you will find that you will soon have a fresher outlook on life. If for those few moments, none of the ills on the edge of your circle pull you away from your center, then you can make it such that they never do. By focusing on being centered on a daily basis, you are creating a new sequence of events that will keep you rooted in the present—you are sending out positive thoughts and actions that will return to you as positive reactions. Now you are aware, mindful and spiritually evolving.

My Practice in Positivity

I can think back to a time not long ago when I felt the weight of my life bearing down on my shoulders. The loss of my son opened the floodgate to other past ills I hadn't fully processed. I looked back on my childhood and found little to smile about. As a child, I recalled loneliness and isolation, low self-esteem, fights with my peers, and battling Attention Deficit Disorder at a young age. In high school, I thought I had my self-esteem in check, but I had unknowingly replaced it with egotistical false perceptions. These carried me to adulthood where I replaced my needs, wants, and desires with co-dependent solutions. After much focused self-reflection, I now have a good grasp of what has afflicted me at an emotional level in my life. This knowledge allows me to better understand myself, but this awareness was only one part of my journey—confronting my ego and false-self was the real battle.

As I looked back, my entire life wasn't a train wreck of pain, drama, and suffering. I could name good friends and loving family members. I always found good memories in my travels and vacations abroad. Still, something was not right. Many times I was overwhelmed by my unhappiness with work and life in general. At times it all felt cruel and unfair. It was easy for me to blame others for my dissatisfaction. I had so many conflicting emotions and thoughts racing through my head. I felt a little lost in the chaos of civilization and found it hard to feel like I was an individual and not just a product of society. I was stuck in a cycle of wake up, work, and come home. I worked hard to barely move my mountain of debt and living expenses. All of these negatives—my childhood, my job, and my unhappiness—became who I was. "Is this it? Is this as good as life gets?" Such experiences dictated how I engaged with life and with others. It was clear I needed a change, but how? I felt trapped and knew I was unhappy, but I had no cure for my seemingly mediocre life. At times it was all incredibly oppressive and overwhelming. Doctors would prescribe anti-depressants, but medicine only dulled the pain, hiding the true sources of my suffering. After the loss of my first child, I begged the Universe to show me a better way out. Having already lost faith in God, I pleaded with the skies above to awaken me to something better.

I'm not sure what really happened.... Some of it is hard to put into eloquent words. I guess you could call it an epiphany or awakening. It happened while I was driving on a long-distance trip years ago in autumn. Strangely, I often think clearly while driving in the middle of nowhere. I think having nothing to focus on but the road allows my mind to relax and sharpen with clarity. On this drive in particular, I was struck by my surroundings. It was an especially sunny day, and the light hit the geography of the land in such a way that everything looked like it had a discernible aura surrounding it. Everything was bright, resolute, and glowing. For a moment, I felt like I was in another world or a dream perhaps. The hum of the road reminded me that I was lucid. As I settled into the present moment, an acute level of clarity washed over me. Even though I still felt trapped by my life and obligations, for a minute or so, I felt really good for no apparent reason. Feeling good was intoxicating. I felt alive and hopeful. I grinned for no apparent reason. Even my stresses, fears, and pressures seemed insignificant and negotiable. My mind was clear and aware. Purely by accident, or maybe because I'd asked for a way out, I found a spiritually meditative connection to my surroundings that brought me a feeling of space and peace. Where did this come from?

Despite my shallow self-worth and depression, I suddenly felt like everything was going to be alright. A day or two after my experience, I went surfing down at a beach close to my home. It was a beautiful Indian summer day. White puffy clouds floated lazily in the unseasonably warm blue sky. A light breeze rustled the leaves of the nearby palm trees. The ocean was a sea of diamonds in the sun. Without even knowing it, I had an acute awareness of my surroundings. As I floated in the ocean waiting for waves, I felt connected and present again. I felt myself floating there in the ocean and at the same time I saw myself from afar, partially blinded by the dazzling sun reflecting off the sea. There was all this space inward and outward. I find it difficult to explain with words, but there was this warm glow that permeated my being. There was so much boundless space surrounding me that I felt protected; that everything was going to be okay. Even my fear of death dissolved because I knew my energy was indestructible. How did I know this? I made a space in my mind for my problems and stresses, but I also made a space for this feeling of peace I felt out on the water. Then I settled into that peaceful space and felt the beauty of the coastline and a connection to something sublime. I could not put my finger on the source of this energy and peace. It felt as though it was welling up from inside, but there was an indescribable essence to it. Instead of trying to analyze this feeling of wellness, I surrendered to its simplicity and radiance. I felt light, free, and resilient. I actually felt lucky to be alive and part of something so beautiful and connected. It was a complete transformation from my previous mood. Soon though, I lost the connection to this space of peace and bliss. Much like a cloud can quickly obscure the sun, I felt preoccupied with the static of my life again. I was no longer mindful of my body, thoughts, or surroundings. It was so easy for random thoughts to enter my mind and close off my space and peace. Yet, in that space I'd made inside my mind, I had the knowledge that I had discovered a meditative way to relax and focus on the positive for just a moment. Within this mysterious space, I connected to my True Nature. What if I could stretch that moment? What if I could live in it?

I began to make it my focus to incorporate this new daily life practice into my regular life. I figured at this point, what could I lose? Further, there were certain subtleties and synchronicities that nudged me into this new direction. Later that week, I took a walk and focused on my breathing and tried to find that connection once more. I focused on nature again, since that seemed to be my gateway. If only for a spare minute, I would glance around my neighborhood and study the leaves on trees, the vivid blue sky, and the scent of jasmine that was in the air. Had that always been there? I began noticing details within my environment that before seemed smoothed over and uninteresting. It was a bit like seeing 20/20 for the first time. Centered in the present, my mind calmed and then a strange and unfamiliar voice spoke. It was my voice, but free from fear and uncertainty. I had never heard it before, but I liked its resonance. It was a voice free from ego and false perception, speaking to me from my True Nature, my source of instinctual energy. How did I know this? I just understood it as a truth from within. It felt right... It made total sense... As I continued to make time to find this connection within my surroundings, this voice continued to speak. This voice brought clarity to my problems and challenges. When I listened and worked to bring about positive outcomes, my fear and anxiety lessened.

This was the merger of heart and mind. When I settled into the present, mindful and boundless, my thoughts were unfettered and free; beyond fear and fantasy. I was connected to the present—this strange world that is a mere blink of an eye between the oppressiveness of ego, fear, and fantasy. I realized that this new voice of perception was my inner wisdom reaching out like a blooming flower, like a well overflowing with fresh pure water to satiate my thirst to evolve.

Months after the loss of John Jr., I embarked on a long and vigilant voyage to cultivating more positive mental states and in my life. These meditations in nature and mind calmed me so that I could think clearly about my life and the misery that seemed to have its gnarled fingers in a chokehold around my neck. I was able to make space for the issues that nagged me and also space for solutions. I realized I had to strip down everything I had learned, from role models to religion, and to rebuild my belief systems from the foundation up. The knowledge and energy I had from the past were not serving me well anymore. Through all the pain and suffering came a new level of self-awareness and inspiration. I was able to acknowledge my weaknesses and not blame others for my mediocrity. I knew I couldn't change my life overnight, but I did know that if I had the patience and persistence, I could begin to move forward instead of standing still, stuck. For once in my life I realized that everything I needed from empowerment and happiness to God was already inside me. I just needed to find the space and the clarity that would allow for this new world to come into focus. In hindsight, what was most empowering about this experience or awakening was that it was not a priest, pastor, or Bible passage that showed me hope and illumination. This empowerment came from within, from my True Nature—an energy center that exists in all of us. It was then when I realized that religion and other dogmas became excessively impractical and unnecessary. Knowing this, dogmatic guilt dissolved and a renewed spiritual confidence bubbled up from within.

These small victories inspired me to try a bigger challenge. For one year, I vowed to work to replace all the negative thoughts I had in my head with positive ones. I knew it would not be a perfect system but the point was to move forward and not backward. I worked on being centered in daily life. I promised to teach myself to live with an open mind and accept the mysterious energies of the Universe. Of course back then, I didn't fully understand the power of positive energy or the notion of True Nature, but the small victories I achieved through my meditations gave me the faith that happiness existed out there for me if I paved a way for it to find me. With mindfulness comes little hints and nudges whether they are thoughts, feelings, or synchronicity within your surroundings. Whatever the signs are, I consider them gifts from the Universe. The art in life is recognizing such gifts and paying heed to their energy and wisdom. Of course at times, I doubted my new resolution and even felt silly, but I pushed on, determined to follow the signs and train my mind to think positively.

As I continued this discipline, I began to sleep better. I had a desire to eat healthier foods and exercise. Becoming mindful of the present made me realize I had no control over the past or even the future, but I did have control over the present by how I met challenges and made decisions. Once this realization hit, I began crafting a new environment from which I could take charge of my present with openness and awareness. When I woke up, instead of focusing on all the tasks I needed to do, I focused on how lucky I was to have a job and how important my role actually was in my office. On my way to and from work, I made a point to stop and appreciate something I found beautiful, whether it was a person, the sun streaking through the branches of a tree in the morning, or the smell of wet pavement after a summer rain. Spending these tiny amounts of time reflecting on positive things was enough to keep the momentum flowing in the right direction. I found that I was more relaxed and able to think more clearly and constructively. I became very aware of the concept of space. It was from space I found clarity and responsiveness.

With a newly opened mind, I hungered for more knowledge and found that Buddhism and eastern philosophies spoke to my new sense of self and awareness. I liked the concepts of karma and self-discovery. They made sense to me. I realized I was not alone in my struggle with breaking free from mediocrity and finding greater meaning in my life. Always a man of science, I gravitated towards studies of quantum physics and how it relates to humans and society. I learned from authors and philosophers who toiled with the same questions and musings. Through regular study and discipline, I found my center. At the end of the day, I mentally praised myself for what I had accomplished and took time to appreciate the positive actions of those around me. I learned to live with compassion and humility. At first, it was difficult and took great focus and effort, but the results were amazing. Through positive manifestation, I was rewriting a negative sequence of events and yielding creative energy that was returning to me in feelings of happiness, positive reactions from others, and a new appreciation of my surroundings. From this positive energy came wellness, betterment, and even financial success. I have now continued this practice for over twelve years. It was from my internal struggles and subsequent liberation that this book was born.

I must confess that portions of this journey were not easy. Of course, there were times when I would lose my concentration or slip back into the controlled (or at least somewhat limited) chaos of life. Still, once recognizing that True Nature is a fundamental component of our being, I knew sanctuary and liberation were not far away. The Nyams or "fits of brilliance" or energy I spoke of earlier are great indications that you are on the right path. I just needed be mindful and reunite myself with the present moment. This is an extensive process and by no means a perfect one. Sometimes events in the day would throw me off-center. I would feel stressed, rushed, or inferior due to low self-esteem. Finding awareness that low self-esteem and ego are false perceptions allows a negative feeling to disappear. When we realize that fear, false-self, and ego are all distorted reflections of our True Nature, such negative feelings have nothing to cling to. Whatever the situation is, I know my anxiety or fear is a sign I need to step back and focus on space and beauty. I need to create a gap between the past and future; I need to focus on my breathing and become more mindful of the present. This always brings back my mind-body connection: By being connected to the present and centered, mends that mind-heart rift that many times is the root of our suffering. Then the negative fog dissipates. I am able to think clearly again and make better, more self-directed decisions to remedy the issues that cause me unhappiness.

The Eighth Mandala

The laws of karma govern positive and negative effects in our environment. Positive reactions are the common denominator of our Universe. Becoming open to the positive energy in nature, beauty, and love is crucial to self-evolution. Focusing on positivity creates waves of joy and healing which will ultimately pulse through our thoughts and actions to build a better life. Understanding this energy means grasping the notion that it connects us all and that we have a responsibility as humans to live well for ourselves and others. Positive energy can help you find your center and make strong, self-directed decisions.

Furthermore, this connection to the Universe's positive energy is the key to linking oneself to the creative forces of the Cosmos and feeling one with the divine. I particularly like how the Eighth Mandala offers a solution to one of the most common mind-heart rifts—desire and reason. Not only does this chapter offer scientific reasoning to explain the mysterious laws of karma and positive energy, it also allows one to put action to intention in a way that will yield joyful results. If we allow the logic and reasoning of the laws of karma to guide our desires and intentions, we can't help but make centered, responsive, and responsible actions within this web of energy and life that connects us all.

Eighth Mandala Exit Strategy

- Be aware of karma and its cause and effect.
- We can create and receive positive energy.
- Find connections with nature and energy through "energy vortexes."
- Embark on a walking meditation.
- Learn to center your energy throughout the day.

- Meditative awareness of our intentions. Remember, you can meditate anywhere and at any time!
- Mantra: "Breathe in positive energy, breathe out good karma and credibility."
- Daily Life Practice: Be aware of intention, which leads to action.
- Explore bio-energy therapy and learn to heal yourself.

The Ninth Mandala

Confronting Reality Leads to Self-Actualization

Responsiveness

Imagine yourself standing at a metaphorical crossroad in life. Behind you sits the past with all its dogma, social trappings, and control patterns. Ahead sits the future: Unclear and sometimes foreboding. Yet, here you are firmly rooted in the present—aware, mindful, and with destiny sitting in the palm of your hand.

The Ninth Mandala is the circle that binds together all of the previous Mandalas. It involves using your own power to transform the quality of your life. It requires us to be mindful of the present—this surreal blink of an eye that is your center of existence surrounded by the past and future. Once centered, you will find unadulterated wisdom to revisit your personal beliefs. You need courage to look back on your past and understand why you are hardwired to react certain ways. More importantly, you need strength and diligence to break the control patterns that influence your behaviors. In order to foster this faith, courage, and strength, you must nurture your body through healthy eating, regular exercise, meditation, and relaxation. Find true love and embrace it. Understand karma and learn how to channel the Universe's healing energy into your own life and into the lives of those around you. Then, the future will no longer look foreboding and unclear. Much as clouds can obscure the blue sky, with the right focus and diligence you can walk confidently forward, centered in the present with the sun shining brightly on your back, lighting your true path forward to self-actualization.

One of the most pressing problems with the Ninth Mandala is identifying the more poignant questions to ask and then opening up oneself for the answers. There are many who are lead by blind faith, unfortunately never mindful enough to ask the right questions; still others may ask but be fearful of the answers. When we connect to our True Nature, the intrinsic, immortal potential for reaching enlightenment that exists in all of us, we gain confidence beyond ego and such questions will eventually be answered from your internal source of instinctual energy—your inner voice. As you move through the Mandalas with great diligence, you will begin to ask the right questions and seek the right answers that will help you define a new reality, your "True Reality," framed by your own life experiences and authentic thoughts and opinions. It is then that you can engage fully in the ever-changing, chaotic social world, with more freedom from ego and false-self. You can take up new responsibilities and feel a refreshing glow as you observe the world with your new, focused vision. The differences you perceive in the world and in yourself will be amazing. You will no longer live under a veil of uncertainty and passive fear. You will be conscious of your energy levels and how they fluctuate throughout the day. You will be mindful of the thoughts continually streaming through your mind. You will be intuitive about other people and their energy. You will be more rooted in the present. You will have a healing touch. You will have achieved a form of self-actualization.

The Ninth Mandala is about interacting in this world with a whole new level of responsiveness. We have discussed in depth the need to be open to change and new perceptions. The Universe, the mind, and True Nature are inestimable and interconnected at all imaginable levels. Possessing and wielding these inward and outward qualities of space instills minfulness and creative freedom. With this comes confidence and clarity in life. Responsiveness takes this one step further. By living and acting within the spacious qualities of the mind as it relates to our True Nature, we observe that we are part of something so vast and special, its qualities transcend this ordinary existence we call life, the "material world." With this great awareness comes great diligence to stay centered in this spaciousness so that we can continually be in a place in our minds where we have the greatest depth and profundity. This practice of being mindful of ourselves and our exterior surroundings is responsiveness. It allows us to connect to ourselves and to our environment and people around us by channeling our flow of positive energy inward and outward, a projection or manifestation of positivity. This is the Responsive Universe: Being aware of ourselves and others, our thoughts and our actions, in a karmic way that involves an awareness of our control patterns and True Nature so that we may act in ways authentic to ourselves, with the goal of evolving socially and spiritually.

Self-actualization at its apex is enlightenment. The greatest way to achieve this level of understanding ourselves is to reach out to others and our Universe with love and compassion. Just as we can reach an understanding of the Universe and its fundamental laws of physics through study and hypothetical thought processes, we can come to a great understanding of our lives in much the same way. We analyze the creation of the Universe according to a sequence of precise events across a timeline. Likewise, we can retell the narratives of our lives in a similar way to see the truth in our childhoods and see through the negative control patterns, pain, and loss in order to reach the gates of understanding and illumination. The way to develop this responsive vision and keep it intact, to realize, feel, and draw in the world's beauties and energies, is simply to love.

Universal Love

Universal love is not about sexual lust, infatuation, or even the deep love you feel for a spouse or child. The definition of universal love is much like that of True Nature—it is almost indefinable because it encompasses everything. Language fails when trying to say what universal love means in words, but we have all had those moments when what we feel is so strong that we can't find words to describe it. Our emotions could write books but our brains can't seem to put such energy into words. We might not have the verbal language to describe these moments, but we do have the capacity in our hearts and minds to comprehend this level of energy. This energy is what makes the Responsive Universe operate. It is the unwritten law around which the world revolves. It flows through everything from a star in the night sky to a tiny seedling in your front yard. This is love at its most common denominator. Love is creation. Love is the essence of God. Love is birth and death as it flows through life in ever-changing form. Love is the ultimate positive action we can take that sends streams of positive reactions into the world. Quantum Physics explain love as sub-atomic energy connected to everything. Love is energy in every particular reality and it cannot be destroyed. It exists in some form or facet in our bodies, our minds, and in the Universe forever. Why not connect more to this dynamism?

Happiness

A key element to self-actualization and positive healing energy is raising one's emotional baseline of happiness. This level of happiness is not like the conventionally defined emotion that means satisfaction and pleasure in the present moment. An emotional baseline of happiness should remain constant, much like True Nature. For many of us, our emotional baseline can diminish or intensify according to current situations, but such peaks and valleys ultimately even out, leaving you with your baseline yet again. Developing a greater awareness for our emotional baseline and working to be more responsive in our lives can increase the positive energy we generate and feel, thus increasing our happiness. Happiness is not brought about by wealth and things. A good meal, a cold beer, a fast car, an amusement-park ride—all of these things will make you feel great for a moment—but none of them will bring you a lifetime of happiness. It is great to enjoy the nice things around you, but we must not attach our well-being to these transitory things.

The Dalai Lama, when asked what surprised him most about humanity answered,

"Man. Because he sacrifices his health in order to make money. Then he sacrifices money to recuperate his health. And then he is so anxious about the future that he does not enjoy the present, the result being that he does not live in the present or the future. He lives as if he is never going to die, and then dies having never really lived."

Everything you need to be happy is already inside you: The essence of God, True Nature, and love. Even better, these three ideals are actually synonymous with each other; you need only make the space in your mind to marry them into one and be in synch with positivity and creation. In order to tap into this emotional baseline and even raise it to increase happiness, we must make an honest attempt to erase our false-selves and connect to our True Nature. Happiness is not easy. Just like the concept of self-actualization and enlightenment, it takes dedication and diligence to stay centered, focused, and responsive. Just think—if everyone worked towards this goal of authenticity and happiness, there would be so much less suffering in the world as a whole.

At times, you may feel lost in your efforts. It may seem that your efforts in the grand scheme of things do very little to increase our collective happiness across the globe. Instead of despairing at these times, let those moments be a trigger to push forward even harder. We are here on this planet to work together, not against each other. Find hope in knowing that your actions, no matter how small they may seem, do make a difference and that they also set an example for those around you. As particle physics now shows, we are connected at many unseen levels. Our actions, no matter how small, do change the fabric of the Universe. We are all connected, as are our actions, reactions, emotions, and manifestations. Why wouldn't we want to root our actions, needs, wants, and desires to our True Nature and free them from the perils and suffering of ego and false-self? You alone have the power; creation and opportunity sits within your heart and mind, married as one entity.

No matter what challenges we may face, there is a way to make a profound impact on the intensity of happiness within our lives. You can just start by becoming more mindful of your emotional responses to people and situations. This not only increases our awareness, it also increases our responsiveness. Becoming more aware of our positive, negative, and neutral reactions to what we are facing gives us a stronger sense of our emotional baseline. Breaking negative control patterns that alter reactions to our life contexts will allow us to raise our emotional baseline. Much like our true selves, we can free our happiness from anchors of past traumas, false perceptions, and low self-esteem. This requires much vigilance and concentration, but the hard work and dedication yields tremendous results. The secret to being happier is not the acquisition of things we desire; it is in shedding all the trappings of our false-self and negativity that weigh our emotional baseline down. Being happy is being responsive. Responsiveness needs space, not clutter.

"Follow your bliss and the Universe will open doors where there were only walls."

Joseph Campbell

Our world appears to operate by money, charisma, and power. Happiness, however, can be found in this confusing world. What is vital in our search for satisfaction is defining happiness for ourselves and always determining its source—whether this happiness is genuine to us or whether we have allowed others to define it for us. These are difficult things to ponder, but these mental explorations are what spur our evolution into higher functioning individuals. The first eight Mandalas address the three elements that constitute a complete person: Body, mind, and True Nature. Mindfulness, health, and love all put us in touch with these elements, allowing us to channel positive energy into our lives and create actions that increase our energy levels and responsiveness. But we have to decide to be positive and responsive individuals. All of that effort, backed by our compassion and courage, comes from the power of our heart and mind, merged as one. Only you have the power to make these lasting transformations in your life. Therefore, you alone hold the key to happiness. The choice is yours…

The mind is similar to any muscle in your body. The more you use it, the stronger and more efficient it becomes. The brain's best exercise is education, experience, and introspection. The mind will grow stronger by simply dedicating yourself to meditation and positive thinking. Generating your own answers to life's questions is essential to your self-directed future. As you ponder your past, you may continue to believe the things you were taught as a child, or you may cast them off and develop new world views. The Ninth Mandala is about this vigilance: To strive to use your own mind and senses as filters to your life experiences and continually to peel away anger, envy, self-doubt, all of the traps of the ego that keep you from being actively and authentically responsive.

When it all becomes too much, always remember to take a pause. Try to relax. Find space for your troubles and musings. Please recall that it is from space that awareness and clarity arise. To think constructively, you must be relaxed. Find your center and attune yourself to the present moment. Pull inspiration and energy from your surroundings. Focus on the horizon at the time that the sun is setting over the ocean. Sit on a lush hill and look out over a fertile valley. Sit on a rooftop and take in the night time cityscape. Listen to a piece of music that transports you to a dreamscape. Breathe deeply. Hold in the precious air and slowly exhale. Focus on creation. Focus on beauty. As you relax, you can make your mind focus on anything. Observe that power. Use that power to see past your problems and worries and uncover the roots of these woes. Be the author of your own parables. Determine constructive ways to deal with them. Pen a positive future. You have the ability to slow down, focus your mind, and use its power to determine plans and answers that will pave your way toward self-actualization.

Awaken yourself

Humanity has been on the verge of a collective awakening for thousands of years. Great teachers dating back to the Buddha, Aristotle, Plato, or, more recently, Joseph Campbell, Eckhart Tolle, and the Dalai Lama show us this metaphysical world where every reaction is governed by action. A world where karma creates our events and destiny, and where energy is the paying currency here, now, and hereafter. Quantum Physics is now revealing our kinship at the sub-atomic level. Meditation shows us another view of this connected world, free of false-self, unadulterated and liberated, a new voice emerges… your inner wisdom, speaking truths, birthing your epiphany of existence. This is what it means to be awake, and this state of being, this non-duality, is the next evolutionary goal for humanity.

Now, with the internet, social media unites this new renaissance in thinking and expression. This dissemination of energy and wisdom is catching on like wildfire to a dry field of wheat; our once stale, dogmatic world is ablaze as the flames of enlightenment ignite the embers of our being. We are all now connected to the great teachers, poets, and champions of enlightenment. Information is now available so that the collective world can weed out the truths and fallacies that surround us. With understanding comes less fear of the unknown. There is this new pulse reverberating outward. As we breathe in and become mindful of our inner and outer surroundings we draw in this energy and wisdom, thus creating our own ideas of the why and how. The more awake you become, the larger your energy footprint becomes... To be awake is to understand universal love and wisdom. Fear dissolves and empowerment sits at your fingertips. You might not be able to explain it eloquently (many try, including me) but deep down you know the truths of our connection to energy and Universe. You can feel this connection. You understand that everything is going to be okay. Words may not be able to describe such feelings, some of which can be fleeting to those fresh to this new world. Still, for those that have awakened, each will have their story to tell, their own path and interpretations, and yet the common denominator will be the same. Our paths come from different places but the journey always leads to the same destination: Self-actualization...

Why are so many missing the bigger picture? Why aren't more people awakening? That question might be more complex than the social conditioning that shapes each of us. Ego would be the biggest barrier that creates so many control patterns in our short impressionable lives that it is too easy to grow old unknowingly missing the gifts that have been there all along. Ironically the trimmings and frills we thought were important and brought us happiness at a younger age may not be satiating our desire to evolve at a more mature age. The "material world" we were born into does not mesh well with the "True Reality" your inner wisdom craves. Evolution is slow and tedious, as reflected by our own world. Humans are championed by our greatest discoveries and achievements and we are at the same time horrified by the war, famine and persecution that still plagues Earth today. How do we make any sense of it? In any case, the bright light of energy, wisdom, and love cannot be extinguished. The essence of our True Nature is indestructible and always present. Everything you need to unlock life's most intriguing questions resides in your heart. Yearn to awaken to this wisdom; be mindful of the gifts awaiting you and this increasingly expansive Responsive Universe we all live in. Be a pioneer in your own journey to self-discovery and set an example for others to follow.

Meditation Session

Daily Energy Therapy

Following the pattern of previous meditation sessions, find a quick few solitary minutes away from the hustle and bustle of life where you will not be interrupted. You can do this exercise lying down, sitting in a chair, or even standing up. As we have done before, take deep breaths into your lower abdomen. With each deep breathe, hold it and count to five before slowly releasing the air out of your lungs and body. As you inhale, visualize positive energy flooding into your body. As you exhale, visualize negativity, stress and disease leaving your body. Do this about 5-10 times. Sometimes it takes longer to relax the body and mind and additional rhythmic breathing may be required. A noticeable change in energy levels will be apparent in about 5 to 10 minutes. As always, be aware of your constant streaming of positive, negative, and neutral thoughts from within. Determine if you feel centered in your "circle of energy" (as we discussed in the Eighth Mandala). A good time to do this exercise is in times of stress or when you simply feel overwhelmed or low on energy. In just minutes, you will feel more energetic and alive, ready to meet the challenges of the day with more liveliness.

Daily Life Practice

As we have learned, meditation is a great tool for calming the mind and introducing positive mental imagery designed specifically to leave lasting imprints on the conscious and subconscious mind. We also talked about focusing on nature and its positive benefits. By simply being aware of our surroundings and the beauty and energy they offer, we can raise our emotional baselines through daily practice. We talked earlier about different exercises which can help raise that emotional baseline, and about exercises like meditation, daily life practice, or merging heart and mind and incorporating more happiness into your daily life. After you finish this book, please stay diligent with your meditation and daily life practices. Just because you finished this book does not mean you should stop your practice. This includes connecting the mind with body. Focusing on good health and exercising should be a continual part of our evolving life.

Have you found any early benefits from following the guided meditations and daily life practices presented here? I bet you have new perspectives on life. Have your perceptions of the world developed—both in regard to your mind and the vastness of True Nature and how it relates to the Universe? If you said yes to any of these questions then you owe it to yourself to continue with meditation and daily life practice. Clearly you are evolving as a human beyond the normal toils of life. Search out new books and maybe join a class on Buddhism or Zen meditation. Your journey is just beginning and yet you have come so far already. Do not let mediocrity and false perception ever rule your life again. Be strong and aware—find openness in life and revel in the magnificence of our Responsive Universe. Focus on your continued evolution into self-discovery.

Enlightenment

Siddharta of the Gautama clan was born in approximately 563-483 BCE. He was to become more widely known as Shakyamuni (sage of the Shakya tribe) and especially as the Buddha (the Awakened One).

The Shakyas were the kshatriya (warrior/governing/aristocratic) caste of the city-state of Kapalivatthu, in a region located somewhere along what is now the India-Nepalese border. Siddhartha's father, Shuddhodana, one of the leaders of Kapalivatthu, is sometimes represented as being a king (with Siddhartha termed a prince, and his mother, Mahāmāyā, similarly given the title of queen), although the city-state was more precisely a republic than a kingdom in the modern sense.

In any case, Siddhartha grew up in material and emotional comfort, the story tells us, living in relative luxury, enjoying life and fully protected and blinded from its more harsh features. We learn that on Siddhartha's 29th birthday, on the fifth full moon of the year, he came to certain sudden realizations concerning the existence of aging, sickness, and death, which radically transformed his sense of life and propelled him to go forth in a profound spiritual search. At that time, he wandered away from his life's protective walls (both physically and metaphorically speaking) to see what life was like outside his home. Walking through the nearby village, he saw a diseased man, a decaying corpse, and a religious man who, by some accounts, was fasting. Having never seen suffering or death before (the story goes), Siddhartha set off on a quest to know and understand. He gave up his comfortable life and began to travel. Over the course of several years, he became a beggar, a student, and an ascetic. Six years later and after a reputed final 49 days of meditation under a Bodhi tree, Siddhartha became enlightened. This is said to be the night of his 35th birthday. From that time on, he became known as the Buddha, literally, the "Awakened One."

Whether the story of the Buddha is truth or lore really does not matter. This story of witnessing suffering and then awakening to our true-self is a path we must all eventually walk. There lies the importance and wisdom of this tale. An awakening occurs as the result of an elevation in consciousness, where people become aware of realities and parts of themselves that were previously hidden. The shift in consciousness following an awakening is more or less permanent, as it changes one's outlook on life completely. Being enlightened does not mean that there is no turbulence in yours or others' lives. Suffering still exists on the planet. Enlightenment involves having the space and awareness to avoid attachments like vices and control patterns that link us to suffering. Enlightenment is an awakening of the mind to its original purpose—to love. Atop the surface of the "material world" is True Reality. You can think of enlightenment as a journey. If faced with uneven terrain, most people will desire to walk downhill because it's easier. In order to rise beyond the trappings of the materialistic world, however, you must walk uphill. It is much more difficult to walk uphill, and you may ask, "Why not choose the easier route?" The answer is simple: When you choose to walk uphill and eventually reach the top you gain a perspective that allows you to look down on your life and the world and see everything as a complete picture. You will see how everything fits together. You will understand your suffering and your control patterns because you will see their strains woven into the tapestry of your life you see before you.

Once you recondition your mind to be responsive, the uphill journey won't be as taxing. It is strange that we must suffer a little in order to end our suffering, but the mild suffering we feel as we walk uphill is a trigger that we are on the right path. We are not choosing to be passive participants in life. As the journey gets intense, your false-self and ego will think of countless reasons why you should stop, take a break, turn around, or just sit and rest for a while. The ego can be quite persuasive and will stop at nothing to try to impede your progress using shame and guilt. Once we achieve this new perspective, however, new horizons open to us in a spacious vision of clarity. You will be refreshed with a new awareness of your surroundings. Life will no longer look complex and confusing. Your thoughts and beliefs will be clearer and more focused, and soon everything you once thought was right (in the "material world") will be a bit blurry and skewed. Your True Reality is a different world that requires a new responsive vision. You don't just see the world as it is; you are the world and all it can become. You are in a place free from ego and fear. The Responsive Universe is an alternative existence. This new world has always been there—false perceptions and ego simply obscured it from your view like dark clouds over a starry night sky.

Non-duality

Non-duality describes a state of being that is void of ego. It is a state where we have settled into the quality that is our True Nature—the natural state of being that had been handed to us at birth, free from outside pressures. When we settle into this state, we are living without the weights of social conditioning, personal history, or any definition of "self" defined by our culture or society. When we settle into this state, self-image disappears because we become aware that the identity we perceived as important before, the one attached to our job, possessions, and reputation, has no foundation. We associated that identity with things and ideas that were transient. Seeking identity from our True Nature, however, means attaching our self-image and esteem to something steadfast and dependable.

As we become awakened, we must be mindful of a new false-self that can develop. We discussed the inner fight we could feel as we shed our false-self and ego and embrace our new world of positive energy and responsiveness. As we continue to evolve, we may begin to see others suffering, mired in ego and fear. We must have compassion for them and support them on their journeys. If you feel superior to them, that is a trigger to you that you are letting your ego do your talking once again. As long as you are immersed in society, the ego will always exist. As you interact with people, remember to be humble. Be mindful of all of your actions and continue to ask yourself if they are rooted in ego or in True Nature.

It is also important in your personal evolution never to lose sight of your origination point. Where were you when you started your journey? Our road to self-actualization and responsive living allows us to move beyond our pasts and mistakes, but we cannot forget them. By remembering them, we ensure that we will not repeat them.

Your entire perspective will change once you settle into the spacious vision that is the Responsive Universe

Remembering them also helps continue to fuel our passion to create new positive reactions in life. Looking back on how our lives were before should fill us with gratitude for how far we have advanced. There is a great wisdom and responsiveness to this idea. Our pasts and mistakes, with our new level of reflection, no longer weigh us down, but allow us to ascend further towards our goals for happiness and fulfillment. They also reinforce the notion that your happiness and the new healthy life you are now leading were created by you alone. Your past no longer makes you feel powerless. Your past is another source of empowerment.

Much of our discussion of the Ninth Mandala consists of matters of the mind. As we shed our false-selves while remaining humble and mindful of our origins, we must also be aware of the body changes that can occur with our awakenings. This great shift in consciousness we experience can open the floodgates to all sorts of sensory experiences that can be greatly felt in the body.

Many practitioners call these manifestations of rising energy levels "Kundalini Symptoms." These signs can differ dramatically from person to person, but very common symptoms include acute sensations of tingling, heat, or cold (often more during meditation or bio-energy healing), slight involuntary movements, mild digestive problems, headaches, rapid mood shifts, hearing inner sounds such as humming or buzzing, sensitivity to light, and a sense of being overwhelmed by this new world. People have also reported psychic experiences such as past-life memories or astral travel, as well as an intense insight and understanding of one's own essence and environment, including an awareness of the energies of others. Others have felt increased creativity, particularly in outlets of self-expression and communication through music and journaling. As with any new experience or feeling, eventually this new energy or dynamism will become a backdrop to new experiences—in essence what was once strange and surreal will be commonplace and appear to be the norm. Other symptoms like headaches or digestion issues will dissipate quickly.

The important thing to remember in the Ninth Mandala is that the more aware and mindful we become, the more aware and mindful we must be of our new energy levels and life changes. We must open ourselves up to all the changes we feel and make space in our minds to live them all fully, allowing the new energy to flow through us and not get stuck in any sensory experiences or whispers from our quieted egos.

As you move through the Mandalas, you will become happier and more centered. You will have an increased, if not masterful, awareness of yourself and your environment. With your more focused vision, you may look back on your life and wonder if you were the same person back then.

You were once molded clay, a product of society and religion, and now you sense that you are your own person—both the art and the artist, slowly born from the constraints and pain that once held you prisoner. You may consider yourself a student right now, but soon you will be a mentor and teacher, either inspired to share your knowledge, or simply to lead by example.

Suffering as it relates to Awakening

Experience has taught with excruciating detail that suffering is an undeniable facet to our being. We now understand that limiting the ego's influence allows for our True Nature to wellspring from within, thus facilitating more happiness and positive energy. We also now understand with certainty that the goal in life is to suffer less and achieve some form of enlightenment or self-actualization. But we do not live in a perfect or enlightened world, do we? No matter how intense or dedicated our efforts to strive for positivity and betterment, challenges and tragedies will still hit us with unflinching force. As the Fifth and Sixth Mandalas explain, certain suffering in life is unavoidable. Situations like child abuse or the loss of a loved one would be examples that are literally out of our control. Some challenges are unforeseen, unpredictable, and many times so intense and devastating that they can change us forever. So is the concept of suffering unavoidable in life? And if so, what is the reason for its existence? Why in a Universe of positive actions and reactions does this type of suffering exist? Here lies another paradox of sorts, maybe even a silver lining in what sometimes seems like completely inescapable situations.

What if suffering is part of our social and spiritual evolution? We now understand that God is not this representation of a man and his omnipresent hand that projects this divine will on who lives to be old and wise and who dies young in a tragedy. As explained in the Third and Fourth Mandalas, God's energy and power sits in the hands of humans; wielding our karma and energy to create a living heaven and or hell here on Earth. The losses we see in life many times are not "divine will" but a source of statistics and probability. I know that sounds cold and surgical but our world, though instinctual and full of energy, is also governed by math. We now understand how quantum physics governs our Universe and thus the concept of God is considered to be all things tangible and intangible—a system of instinctual energy and wisdom as it relates to the Cosmos. We understand that the Universe was born from imperfection, and human suffering may in fact be a facet of this imperfection. Let us not forget that beauty is born from imperfection too. Yet, experience shows us that intense suffering seems to shatter the ego's grasp on our lives, opening us up to the raw and exposed emotions that root to our True Nature. Please remember that our True Nature is everything; beyond ego and false-self. This includes our bliss and happiness and also our pain and anguish as it relates to our present, unadulterated emotions. How are we to fathom love and happiness without knowing its polar opposite: Pain and suffering? Both complex processes seem to operate in a responsive world of cause and effect; a revolving Mandala. These true emotions are connected and seem inseparable, twisting and turning like a wild pendulum born from our experiences.

But why do we have to suffer?

We have discussed how the ego is an inescapable social phenomenon, obscuring our true vision, many times unknowingly. Intense suffering seems to rip the grip of ego away thus revealing our True Nature within. Yes, it can take an unprecedented emotional toll on us and our immediate friends and family; it is as life-changing as it is devastating. Even witnessing the suffering of those we do not know personally can pull at our emotions. Though there always is an exception to the rule; in general humans need to hit rock bottom to reveal to us our inner strengths and wisdom. It takes staggeringly painful experiences to jolt us from the haze of ego and false-self. Only then can new doors open to us that seemed impenetrable before. I know it seems like a very imperfect system of cause and effect but keep in mind our ideals and perceptions are forged from societal immersion and conditioning. As an example, many look to death as a negative experience and yet there is nothing more natural and encompassing. It is something we will all experience and yet there is so much anxiety and fear associated with it. And yet, death may be the most alluring and beautiful of all the seasons in life. Experience has shown that if something is painful enough but it does not kill us, it tends to make us stronger and wiser in the long run. For those few that experience a spiritual awakening, most of the answers materialize as gifts from within (your inner wisdom). Without regular mindfulness and meditation, for most of the human population the closest we get to raw, unadulterated emotions; our true naked self free from ego and false-self; is when we look pain, misery, and suffering directly in the eye. Nothing hurts more and we are never so present in the moment as when experiencing a terrible loss or tragedy.

Looking back on my past reveals several hardships that have only strengthened my resolve. From pain comes a greater mindfulness of what true happiness is and where to find it. Sometimes it is difficult to see the wisdom in such notions. It can seem like a sick joke, but when you detach yourself from the emotional baggage that weighs us all down, when you take ego and dogma out of our thought processes, when you look at life and death as a revolving door of energy, your intense suffering can be a corridor of mindfulness and eventually evolution and self-actualization. Sometimes we need to lose something to gain something else. That thought is very hard to digest when we are faced with a debilitating loss. Yet, years later the fruits of such toil may reveal themselves as something new, inspirational, and empowering. You may think suffering a loss is not worth it (and I agree), but we really don't have a choice here, do we? My own personal hardships have all come at a cost. At times it seems as though a part of you dies. This may be true, but another part of you is born in the process. As I look back on the past tragedies and challenges in my life, I see two veering paths. One is the sadness and suffering, but from that path springs another. My biggest jumps in social and spiritual evolution, my biggest breakthroughs and awakenings from false-self, have always been most powerful after suffering from intense loss or stress.

Let illumination guide you on your new path

The connection is simple. We are born as mortal energy to learn and expand our energy footprint, to live karmic lives, and to understand all facets of existence. This includes the good and the bad. With space and clarity, our suffering can harden our disposition and also awaken our vision. From great sadness and fear can come immense happiness and bliss. The two polar opposites need each other to exist, and knowing one is being intimate with the other. The balance of this experience is space, clarity, and responsiveness—the essence of instinctual energy, wisdom, and love. When we come to bear witness to this paradox, we live life more fully in the now and especially in the hereafter. Loss is not an ending but the beginning of something immense we have yet to comprehend.

Meditation Session

Manifestation Meditation

The Nine Mandalas show us that we have the power to manifest our own creative reality. We now realize that our True Nature is unwavering and is the environment from which the energy of the Universe and God vibrates across an electromagnetic field of actions and reactions. We are connected to this field of energy through body and mind. Knowing this, we can be confident that we belong to the Universe and that the Universe belongs to us. We do not need religious trappings or blind faith to understand that we are part of something greater than ourselves. As we discussed in the Eighth Mandala, we have the ability to harness this great energy around us and inside us and even pass this healing energy on to others. Karma and the power of positive thinking or prayer illustrate this phenomenon. Sub atomic physics scientifically proves this connection.

During this meditation, visualize a blank movie-screen or canvas. As you control your breathing and settle into its deep rhythm, mentally visualize an aspiration. Project this dream onto your minds blank screen or canvas. Fill the empty space with images of you achieving this dream. Keep your mind rooted in the present and try to hold onto this imagery for as long as possible. Draw on the quantum energy of the Universe to make these images stamp a lasting imprint in your mind. Infuse these images with this energy. Feel the energy breathing life into them as your own breath deepens. Feel the energy turning these thoughts into actions, bringing your dreams to life. Remember, every positive thought creates a ripple of energy, altering the fabric of the Universe in some facet. The more ripples you create the more energy you manifest.

The caveat to this exercise is to project images that are practical and karmic, dreams that actually meet your natural needs and aren't the wishes of our ego. You can't visualize being a billionaire for the sole purpose of being filthy rich. Align your dreams with your heart's true wish. Make sure your dreams fulfill your goals of self-growth and personal evolution. All of your dreams should be rooted in happiness.

Another caveat to this exercise is to be mentally prepared to accept your manifestation when it materializes. You must become aware and responsive enough to recognize its presence. For example, you may be dreaming of seeing your art works in a gallery. If you are only focused on finding a gallery, you may miss meeting a stranger on the subway who knows a gallery owner. You may miss the flyer you see at your local farmers' market calling for rising artists to gather in the park the next weekend for a neighborhood art fair. As you begin to utilize the newfound space in your mind for goals and aspirations, you must also make the space to be open to all the opportunities the Responsive Universe brings you.

This is a very effective exercise and with diligence and repetition, your dreams can become a reality. This book was published from a projected manifestation within my own mind. For months I visualized my writings being published by a wellness publisher—I visualized success. And then I and Wisdom Moon Publishing came in contact with one another and voilà: success! Dreams do come true and miracles do happen. Please, let this book be proof that we can manifest energy to meet our most wonderful dreams.

Daily Life Practice

As we continue to connect to the energy and wisdom of the Mandalas, we focus much of the positive energy we find in ourselves and in the Universe to complete these self-reflective tasks, thus directing almost all of our energy internally. The more authentic and responsive we become, however, the more we need to direct some of our positive energy outside of ourselves. This creates a fruitful relationship of karmic give-and-take between us and our environment. In this daily life practice, think of someone you know who you think needs help. Much like the previous meditation, visualize this person on a blank screen or canvas. Breathe in positive energy and imagine you are storing this energy inside your chest. Feel the energy build and glow within you. Feel your heart and mind merge as one. Feel warmth and positivity permeate from your aura. Then send this energy to the person you have in mind. See the person in your imagination and feel the warmth and power leave your body and enter his or hers. Repeat this exercise several times to create a vivid mental imprint and energy exchange. Feel positive energy return to you as you send it out. As much energy you send out, you receive back from the Universe, your source of infinite karmic quantum energy. Remember, based on simple quantum physics, we are all energy and the act of observing or manifesting this energy changes its form or direction based on our confidence and intention.

The Ninth Mandala

The Ninth Mandala is about responsiveness. Responsiveness comes with great responsibility—both to ourselves as we continue on our paths to self-actualization, and also to the Universe as a whole as we finally come to appreciate—with our own eyes and heart, separate from religious or societal edicts—that we are part of something vast and amazing. As we become aware of our own personal histories and the achievements and failures that impress and haunt us, we must take time to reflect outwardly at our world's history.

What triumphs and atrocities world-wide impress and haunt us? We have discussed the two paths that we as individuals can take as we contemplate our goals of self-actualization. The first path, the easier one, is idleness. This path ensures our own lives will be mediocre at best, as we at most barely live to our potential; in this way we never fully understand what our personal potential actually is. A society of individuals all traveling this path leads to great global strife, suffering, and conflict. This is the path where the ego runs rampant. Unbridled egos bring internal wars within the self, many times unknowingly. Globally, they bring political unrest, religious persecution and discord, terrorism, poverty, and famine. Imagine hundreds of people wrestling with control patterns and egos that prevent them from making authentic, responsive decisions and actions. Imagine thousands. Imagine millions. This kind of society can only succeed in decreasing the quality of life for its members. Please be mindful of this.

The second path, however, is one paved by us, the rebellious ones who rise above the static of society in pursuit of personal and global happiness. We are the "Light Workers," who ironically work the hardest to discover and nurture the light—the blissful intentions and creative forces—that elevates self as well as social awareness. This is a path of education, prosperity, freedom, health, and longevity. This is the path of scientific discoveries and enlightenment. Through self-reflection, we become aware and redirect the hardwired distortions of life. By breaking negative control patterns, we create new positive actions that replace the negative ones. Imagine how much more fulfilling and free your own life is without ego and control patterns weighing you down all the time. Imagine a refreshing new life, free from passive suffering, with happiness the common denominator. Imagine your newfound happiness. Imagine hundreds of people realizing their potential and power as responsive, accountable beings. Imagine thousands. Imagine millions. This second path leads to the continuation of our evolution as an intelligent species. Achieving self-actualization is our responsibility as responsive social beings who wish for personal and global happiness. It is our evolutionary goal as social and spiritual creatures.

The Illumination of the Nine Mandalas

When we pause, breathe, and live in the silence of our thoughts and True Nature, there is this sublime dynamism that links us to something so vast and magnificent it completely boggles the imagination. The aperture of our open mind allows us as conscious, instinctual energy to connect to something not just grand, but incomprehensible. Through space and awareness, we mend the rift caused by ego, thus marrying the heart and mind as one.

Welcome to a Responsive Universe!

As authors of our own finale, we see the past and the ache of loss as a source of empowerment, a beginning with the ending still ahead of you yet to be self-actualized. We see that we are part of a system of quantum laws and paradoxes so unfathomable that organized religion seems to be this gratuitous, thin sliver of light obscuring the true gift of energy, illumination, wisdom, and love.

Through meditation and mindfulness we connect to this responsiveness, this bond, these feelings so difficult to capture with scripture or even words. Yet it is this bond, this union, that awakens us to another world: A world of sharpened vision, manifestation, and healing energy. By surrendering our false-self, living healthy, and centering our confidence and intent—driven from compassion and heart wish—we realize we are the hands of creation, humans in an intrinsic connection to this infinite Cosmos; we are the architect to our own happiness and perpetual destiny. When we pause and gaze upon the stars at night, the Universe is not a vast and desolate wasteland of emptiness but is instead a cohesive and breathing organism. You and I are an integral component of this organism, the essence of God and human consciousness linked as one in this Mandala of birth, life, and rebirth, our energy carried forth in this celestial matrix to infinity.

About the Author

You may have reached the end of this book with maybe one question still in your mind? Who is John C. Bader? Who am I, claiming to have battled ego, loss, and self-doubt and risen above my mediocrity to embrace a life of change and happiness? I am just like you. I am just one person. We all suffer in ways that seem intimate to us and our circle of friends and family. As I look into the mirror, I see many facets of suffering. I endured a forgettable childhood. I have fought addiction. I have weathered marital problems. I have lost a child. I have raised two. I know what it feels like to be so lonely you don't feel empty inside, you just ache. I also know what it feels like to find love, triumph, and wonderful happiness. I am one person who reflected on my suffering and used it to feel compassion for others instead of hate. I used my suffering as motivation to change the rooted control patterns in my life and build more positive models that yield positive reactions. I broke my own cycle of dysfunction to ensure I didn't pass it down to my children.

John C. Bader

I am not a Doctor or Psychologist; I am simply aware and mindful. It was my innate suffering that eventually birthed an awakening. Still, I am not perfect and I will continue to battle ego and struggle as we all do, but within my boundless mind is a vision of freedom and bliss. It is a vision that is more than just glimpses of passing brilliance. I know now that the energy and power to be happy and successful are found within. I wrote this book to affirm my own thoughts and experiences on my road to self-actualization. Writing is my outlet. I make no claims to have all the answers to life or that my path to happiness is the only one. The most powerful and authentic answers to your life's questions are those that come from you in your deepest and highest consciousness; a wisdom that combines our most penetrating appreciation of our lives, often called our deepest intuition, and not from religion, society, or someone else's beliefs.

My focus was to ask the tough questions and hopefully help create an environment so that you can find the answers for yourself. God's greatest gift to us is our mind and the energy that surrounds it. And here I am—one person whose mind is very capable of sinking into hate and misery. I could choose that path, or I could choose an uphill journey and pen these Nine Mandalas to enlightenment, in an effort to help others around me. I know I am not alone with my struggles and questions and that is why I wrote this book.

I am one man, but I am one man whose choices now have a lasting positive impression on my family and friends. That is everlasting happiness to me. That is my new vision of my past, my present, and my future. I am the author of my own positive ending. I will pass that happiness down for generations in a life form all its own that will forever expand into the fabric of space and time. Who knows what led to the imbalance of positive to negative in my life on that fateful autumn day when I stopped blaming God and the world for my loss and pain, I awakened into a world where the colors were richer and the wind held an energy that was healing. From that moment on, my past was the nothing from which everything positive came.

I am one man. I am one man of admirable height in a Universe that is vast and limitless. But I now understand that my mind is vast and limitless as well. Again, I make no claims to have all the answers, but I do know one thing: The Universe made me, and I can make the Universe better by connecting to my True Nature. I can make the Universe better by making myself a better person because I am connected to the Cosmos in a web of infinite actions and reactions that are responsive and full of possibility. You can too! I truly believe this is our future and evolutionary goal as conscious humans. Once you realize that you alone hold the key to happiness, your heart and mind merge as one in a union that transcends dogma, ego, and earthly possessions, revealing an infinite, awe-inspiring, and sublime world.

Now it is your turn to find your space and clarity within this grand Responsive Universe…

John C. Bader

Notes

All images used with permission of the copyright holders.

Cover
Front Cover Image:
Stacked Rocks - © Konstantin Sutyagin - Shutterstock.com
(also on back cover and seen throughout the book)
Back Cover Image:
Mandala Image - © mtu1969 - Fotolia.com
(also seen throughout the book)

Introduction
Images:
Spine of the Galaxy Image © MarcelClemens - Shutterstock.com

The First Mandala
1. Stillman Drake, Discoveries and Opinions of Galileo; Anchor Books (1957)
2. Joseph Campbell, The Power of Myth; Anchor Books (1991)
3. Mun Ajaan, The Heart Released courtesy of www.accesstoinsight.org
4. Abraham Maslow, Hierarchy of Needs: A Theory of Human Motivation (1943)
5. Sigmund Freud, The Interpretation of Dreams; Franz Dueticke (1899)
6. Bhikku, Buddhadhasa, The Heartwood of the Bodhi Tree; Wisdom Publications (1996)
7. James Redfield, The Celestine Vision; Warner Books (1997)
8. Eric Berne, Research and Theory, Scripts People Live: Transactional Analysis of Life Scripts; Grove Press By Claude Steiner (1990)
9. Jon Kabat-Zinn - courtesy of www.jonkabat-zinn.com
10. Ralph Waldo Emerson - courtesy of www.quotationspage.com
11. Biehler/Snowman, Psychology Applied to Teaching; Houghton Mifflin Company (1990)
12. Muriel James and Dorothy Jongeward, Born to Win: Transactional Analysis with Gestalt Experiments; Addison-Wesley (1971)

13. Matt Rossano, Supernaturalizing Social Life: Religion and the Evolution of Human Cooperation courtesy of www2.southeastern.edu (2007)
14. Jenny Teichmann and Katherine C. Evans, Philosophy: A Beginner's Guide; Blackwell Publishing (1999)

Images:
Sunbeams - © Julydfg - Fotolia.com
True Nature Sunset Silhouette - © styleuneed - Fotolia.com

The Second Mandala

1. Rigdzin Shikpo, Openness, Clarity, Sensitivity; Longchen Foundation (2000)
2. Abundance Tapestry - Mastering Self, Manifesting Abundance - an article by Evelyn courtesy of www.abundancetapestry.com
3. Geshe Kelsang Gyatso, Eight Steps to Happiness, The Buddhist Way of Loving kindness; First American Edition (2010)
4. David A. Leeming, Kathryn Madden, Stanton Marlan, Encyclopedia of Psychology and Religion; Springer (2009)
5. Ezra Bayda and Charlotte Joko Beck, Being Zen: Bringing Meditation to Life; Shambhala (2003)
6. Charlotte Joko Beck - courtesy of www.brainyquotes.com
7. Sharon Salzberg and Joseph Goldstein, Insight Meditation; Sounds True (2001)
8. Henri Cartier-Bresson - courtesy of www.brainyquotes.com
9. Sun Worship - courtesy of www.paganwiccan.about.com
10. Eckhart Tolle, The Power of Now; Namaste Publishing (1999)
11. Jon Kabit-Zim - courtesy of Mindfulness for Beginners; Sounds True (2012)

Images:
Meditation Image (seen throughout the book) - © Mahesh Patil – Fotolia.com
Meditation Photo - © Yuri Arcurs - Fotolia.com

The Third Mandala

1. World Book Encyclopedia - Definition of Religion courtesy of www.worldbook.com
2. David Hume, The Natural History of Religion; Stanford University (1957)

3. Josiah Royce, The Sources of Religious Insight; Catholic Univ. of Amer. Pr (2001)
4. Sigmund Freud, Exploded Manuscript; York (1927)
5. Carl Sagan, Cosmos; Random House (1980)
6. William J. Kaufmann, Discovering the Universe; W.H. Freeman and Co. (1990)
7. William Poundstone, Carl Sagan: A Life in the Cosmos; Holt Paperbacks (2000)

Images:
Spiral Galaxy - © Lasse Kristensen - Fotolia.com
Evolution of a Flower - © Delphimages - Fotolia.com

The Fourth Mandala
1. Carl Sagan, Cosmos; Random House (1980)
2. C.S. Lewis, The Screwtape Letters; Touchstone (1961)
3. Kevin Williams - courtesy of www.near-death.com
4. Alan Watts - courtesy of www.alanwattsarchive.com
5. The concept of a Kundalini Experience courtesy of www.vijaykumar.com
6. The Council of Nicaea - courtesy of www.islamtomorrow.com
7. The Dead Sea Scrolls - courtesy of www.ibiblio.org
8. Ian Shaw, The Oxford History of Ancient Egypt; Oxford Histories (2002)
9. Schwartz GE, Russek LG., Celebrating Susy Smith's Soul: Preliminary Evidence for the Continuance of Smith's Consciousness after Her Physical Death. Journal of Religious and Psychical Research (2001)
10. Bruce Moen - courtesy of www.afterlife.com
11. Death Experience Foundation - courtesy of www.nderf.org
12. Glen Rein, The Journal of Alternative and Complementary Medicine - courtesy of www.liebertonline.com
13. The Huffington Post, Article: 4 Theories On What Happens When We Die; contributors include: Dr. Bruce Greyson, Robert Lanza, Dr. Ian Stevenson and Dr. Eben Alexander
14. Sunil Mukhi, The Theory of Strings: A Detailed Introduction - courtesy of www.theory.tifr.res.in/~mukhi/index.html
15. NOVA: Universe or Multiverse? (PBS programming)
16. Dr. Brian Weiss, Many Lives, Many Masters; Simon & Schuster (1988)

17. Steve Jobs, commencement speech at the University of Stanford (2005)
18. Deepak Chopra, Life After Death, The Burden of Proof; Harmony Publishing (2006)
19. David Searls - courtesy of www.thinkexist.com
20. Joseph Campbell, The Power of Myth; Anchor Books (1991)
21. Gary Zukav, The Seat of the Soul; Fireside (1990)
22. His Holiness the Dalai Lama and Howard C. Cutler, The Art of Happiness; Riverhead Books (1998)
23. The Holy Bible - Revised Standard Edition; Thomas Nelson & Sons (1952)
24. How Black Holes Work, article by Craig Freudenrich Ph.D. courtesy of www.howstuffworks.com
25. The Hawking Paradox - The Science Channel (televised program)

Images:
Spiritual Awakening - © B-C-designs - Fotolia.co
Question Mark - © Mike Kiev - Fotolia.com
God - © rolffimages - Fotolia.com

The Fifth Mandala
1. His Holiness the Dalai Lama and Howard C. Cutler, The Art of Happiness; New York: Riverhead Books (1998)
2. Discover Magazine, Epigenetics/Darwin and Freud Walk into a Bar, article by Dan Hurley (2013)
3. Herbert Ward - courtesy of www.dreamcatchersforabusedchildren.com
4. Sharon Begley, Train your Mind, Change your Brain; Ballantine Books (2007)
5. Rigdzin Shikpo, Openness, Clarity, Sensitivity; Longchen Foundation (2000)
6. Helen Keller - courtesy of www.zentactics.com
7. Colin C. Tipping, Radical Forgiveness, Making Room for the Miracle; Global 13 Publications (2002)

Images:
Child abuse - © Photosani - Fotolia.com

The Sixth Mandala
1. Joseph Campbell, The Power of Myth; First Anchor Books (1988)

2. Deborah Reber - courtesy of www.lovequoteslibrary.com
3. Kahlil Gibran - courtesy of www.brainyquotes.com
4. "Five Stages of Grief" by Elisabeth Kübler-Ross courtesy of www.ekrfoundation.org

Images:
Father and Son - © Mehmet Dilsiz - Fotolia.com
Heart of Clouds - © radoma - Fotolia.com

The Seventh Mandala

1. A Complete Crash Course to Clean Eating: Fitness Magazine – Article by Jocelyn Voo (2013)
2. Tips to Start an Exercise Regiment, article by Scott H. Young courtesy of www.lifehack.org
3. Donald Jay Grout, A History of Western Music; New York: W.W. Norton & Company, Inc. (1980)
4. Ludwig van Beethoven - courtesy of www.brainyquotes.com
5. His Holiness the Dalai Lama and Howard C. Cutler, The Art of Happiness; New York: Riverhead Books (1998)
6. Richard Garlikov, The Meaning of Love courtesy of www.garlikov.com
7. 101 Relationship Tips - courtesy of www.affirmations-for-success.com
8. Sharon Salzberg and Joseph Goldstein, Insight Meditation; Sounds True (2001)
9. Mark Evans, Suzanne Franzen, Roalind Oxenford Southwater, The Healing Touch; Anness Publishing (2001)

Images:
Fresh Veggies - © Gleb Semenjuk - Fotolia.com
Happy Birds - © Dmitry Pichugin - Fotolia.com
Heart and Mind - © puckillustrations - Fotolia.com

The Eighth Mandala

1. James Redfield, The Celestine Vision; New York: Warner Books (1997)

2. Lama Thubten Yeshe, The Bliss of Inner Fire; Wisdom Publications (1998)
3. A Nobel Torsion Message Over Norway by Richard C. Hoagland courtesy of www.enterprisemission.com
4. Spin in Classical and Quantum Theory by H.C. Corban courtesy of www.journals.aps.org
5. James Redfield, The Celestine Prophecy; New York: Warner Books (1993)
6. Albert Einstein, Relativity: The Special and General Theory; New York: Henry Holt (1920)
7. Rigdzin Shikpo, Openness, Clarity, Sensitivity; Longchen Foundation (2000)
8. Medicine of the Future - an article by Stan M. Gardner, M.D. courtesy of www.selfgrowth.com
9. The Neuromodulatory Basis of Emotion, an article by Jean-Marc Fellous courtesy of www.snl.salk.eu
10. Quantum Mechanics and Some Surprises of Creation, Boris Iskakov - author; Cross-posted from I_UFO, by Glenda Stocks, again by Bill Moore. Scanned from the CONTACT, June 14,1994 courtesy of www.sacred-texts.com
11. A Naturalistic Approach to Buddhist Karma & Rebirth, an article by DT Strain courtesy of dtstrainphilosophyblog.blogspot.com
12. The studies of Dr. Korotkov - courtesy of www.new.korotkov.org
13. Matthew Bortolin, The Dharma of Star Wars; Wisdom Publications, Boston (2005)
14. Page Bryant, Terravision: A Traveler's Guide to the Living Planet Earth; Ballantine Books (1991)
15. Bells Theorem - First published Wed Jul 21, 2004; substantive revision Thu Jun 11, 2009, Stanford Encyclopedia of Philosophy
16. The Dorje - an article by Dan Eden courtesy of www.viewzone2.com
17. Mark Evans, Suzanne Franzen, Roalind Oxenford Southwater, The Healing Touch; Anness Publishing (2001)
18. Spin Doctors: A New Paradigm Theorizing the Mechanism of Bioenergy Healing, an article by M. Sue Benford, R.N., M.A. courtesy of www.journaloftheoretics.com
19. Richard Ellis, Practical Reiki; Sterling Publishing, New York (1999)
20. William Lee Rand, Reiki - The Healing Touch; Vision Publications, Southfield, MI (1991)
21. Tina M. Zion, The Reiki Teachers Manual; Authorhouse, Bloomington, IN (2008)

22. Stenger, Victor J., Bioenergetic Fields; The Scientific Review of Alternative Medicine (1999)
23. A Nobel Torsion Message Over Norway by Richard C. Hoagland courtesy of www.enterprisemission.com
24. Theory of Spin Excitations in a Quantum Spin by Andrew Smerald and Nic Shannon courtesy of www.journals.aps.org

Images:
Sedona - Photo by John C. Bader
Maroon Bells - Photo by John C. Bader
Circle of Energy - Image by John C. Bader

The Ninth Mandala
1. His Holiness the Dalai Lama and Howard C. Cutler, The Art of Happiness; New York: Riverhead Books (1998)
2. Johann Wolfgang Goeth - courtesy of www.brainyquotes.com
3. Joseph Campbell - courtesy of www.brainyquotes.com
4. Shafica Karagulla, Breakthrough to Creativity; Marina del Rey: Books Graphics (1967)
5. Joseph J. Weed, Wisdom of the Mystic Masters; Parking Publishing (1968)
6. Rigdzin Shikpo, Openness, Clarity, Sensitivity; Longchen Foundation (2000)
7. The Teaching of Maha Mudra or Non-Dual Bliss in Buddhism by Tara Springett, M.A. courtesy of www.beliefnet.com

Images:
Hands in the Shape of a Heart Framing the Sun.
© Igor Tarasov - Fotolia.com.
Single Ray of Light Hitting the Ocean.
© John Wollwerth - Shutterstock.com.
Sunset in Hanapepe, HI. Photo by John C. Bader.

CPSIA information can be obtained
at www.ICGtesting.com
Printed in the USA
LVHW090927101021
700049LV00005B/82

9 781938 459283